LITTLE KINGDOMS

LITTLE KINGDOMS

THE COUNTIES OF KENTUCKY, 1850-1891

Robert M. Ireland

The University Press of Kentucky

ISBN 978-0-8131-5312-4

Library of Congress Catalog Card Number: 76-024341

Copyright ©1977 by The University Press of Kentucky

A statewide cooperative scholarly publishing agency serving Berea College, Centre College of Kentucky, Eastern Kentucky University, The Filson Club, Georgetown College, Kentucky Historical Society, Kentucky State University, Morehead State University, Murray State University, Northern Kentucky University, Transylvania University, University of Kentucky, University of Louisville, and Western Kentucky University.

Editorial and Sales Offices: Lexington, Kentucky 40506

CONTENTS

Preface	vii
1. Little Kingdoms	1
2. Little Kings	18
3. The Mad Scramble for Office	42
4. Constitutional Convulsion and Confrontation	60
5. Law and Order	71
6. Court Day	90
7. The Railroad Binge	101
8. Fiscal Chaos	124
9. Conclusion and Postscript	141
Notes	151
An Essay on Sources	173
Index	177

PREFACE

No one can understand the history of Kentucky without appreciating the place of the county in her constitutional, political, and social development. In the nineteenth century Kentuckians exhibited a particular proficiency in the art of creating counties, carving out 100 by 1850 and adding twenty more in the next sixty-two years. Today Kentucky ranks third in the nation in total number of counties and second in number of counties per square mile. Although statistics themselves are sometimes misleading, in the case of nineteenth-century Kentucky, her counties constituted a significance directly proportional to their number.

In an earlier book I examined Kentucky's county courts, in many ways the nucleus of county government. In concentrating on the period of the first and second state constitutions, 1792 to 1850, I made only very general observations about the era that followed. The great influence of the county courts in the daily life of antebellum Kentuckians represented the principal thesis of my endeavor. In this study, I take a broader stance, examining the county in Kentucky during the period of the third constitution, viewing not only the county courts but also officers, internal improvements, crime control, court day, politics, finances, special legislation, and constitutional convulsion and confrontation during the Civil War and Reconstruction.

In 1851 Kentuckians implemented their third constitution, which had been in part brought about because of the deficiencies of the county courts. Its principal reform injected elective politics into that system of government. Antebellum reformers complained that county government operated inefficiently, ineffectively, and in some ways corruptly. But with all the debate and revision, the questions remained: Had the revisers cured the constitutional illness? What impact would the democratic process have on the local constitution? Would the great influence of Kentucky's counties recede or increase during the period of the Civil War, Reconstruction, and the Industrial Revolution? What part would her counties play as Kentucky struggled to cope with the Civil War and the violence that followed it? What would be the relationship of the counties to Kentucky's railroad binge of the last half of the nineteenth century? These are some of the questions I attempt to answer in this study.

Many people assisted me in the completion of this book. I would like to thank particularly my former colleague Dr. Thomas D. Clark and my colleague Steven A. Channing, who read the manuscript and offered many valuable suggestions. A grant from the American Bar Foundation expedited the research.

Librarians and archivists facilitate historical research and in my case the following helped greatly: Jacqueline Bull and Alexander Gilchrist of King Library, University of Kentucky; Lewis Bellardo of the Kentucky Division of Archives and Records; Arthur Lawson and Michael G. Snyder of the Lexington Public Library; and Thomas L. Owen of the University of Louisville Archives. I would also like to thank the staffs of the University of Kentucky Law Library, the Kentucky Historical Society, the Louisville Public Library, the Covington Public Library, the Filson Club, and the National Archives and Records Service, Civil Archives Division, Legislative, Judicial, and Fiscal Branch.

Burton Milward of the Papers of Henry Clay Project, University of Kentucky, and Professor Kenneth Vanlandingham of the Political Science Department, University of Kentucky, shared with me their special knowledge of local history and county government of Kentucky.

My wife, Sandra Boyd Ireland, typed the manuscript and prevented me from establishing the international comma error record. I dedicate this book to her.

LITTLE KINGDOMS

1.
LITTLE KINGDOMS

Theoretically only an arm of state government, Kentucky's counties in reality took on characteristics of semi-sovereignties. Once created, they refused to be abolished, fought with neighboring counties over boundaries, resisted encroachment on their own territories, engaged in internecine struggles over county seats, and besieged the legislature with requests that their own particular problems be ameliorated by special legislation. Such activity not only tended to distract the attention of legislators from the more general needs of the Commonwealth but also contributed to its prevailing condition of localism.

Already possessed of 100 counties by 1850, Kentucky added nineteen more in the next forty years, making it the second most constitutionally subdivided state in the Union per square mile. Kentuckians demanded the creation of new counties for a variety of reasons ranging from the legitimate to the absurd. Perhaps the primary reason was to make the county seat more accessible. A county seat remote from one's residence often made it difficult to transact commercial as well as governmental and legal business.

Most rural Kentuckians depended on horses and roads for transportation, and while horses generally performed well, roads often represented little more than mudbaths. Since county seats usually constituted the commercial and social, as well as governmental, center of a county, the closeness of a rural resident to these communities often bore a direct relationship to his economic and political standing. In 1856, for example, the General Assembly formed Rowan County out of Morgan and Fleming counties to make the county seat more accessible to larger numbers of citizens.[1]

Politics and land speculation also motivated those who petitioned for the creation of new counties. More counties meant additional offices for the politically ambitious. A new county might also represent a gerrymandering to further the designs of a political party. There were always those, too, who wished to honor the memory of a deceased statesman by naming a county after him. The land speculator sought to augment the value of his holdings by making them the center of a new county seat. One such adventurer promised to build a courthouse and dispensed large quantities of whiskey in order to create Carlisle County out of Ballard County in 1886 and thereby increase the worth of his extensive landholdings. Ostensibly seeking to honor his daughter Henrietta, a certain Mr. Egner of Trigg County sought to create a county out of parts of Trigg and Marshall counties only to have his efforts defeated at the polls in 1867 and in the legislature two years later. Opponents accused Egner of trying to convert his largely infertile farm into a county seat and thus sell off town lots at inflated prices. Furthermore, they noted, the proposed county would consist of mostly worthless land and only 400 voters.[2]

Others promoted the establishment of new counties in attempts to escape the policies of existing counties. In one instance, disgruntled farmers from Bourbon, Montgomery, Bath, and Nicholas counties, distressed about the mounting railroad indebtedness of their local governments, unsuccessfully campaigned in 1870 for the creation of the county of Richland. In some cases townspeople sought to make their communities county seats through the creation of new counties. Some living in and about the town of Berea unsuccessfully attempted such a maneuver in 1878.[3]

The proliferation of Kentucky's counties produced problems, many of them economic. Usually legislators took care to provide that the citizens of newly created counties would remain liable for their share of any indebtedness existing in their parent county, although such precaution did not always eliminate further controversy. For example, the Court of Appeals ruled in 1892 that Menifee County continued to be liable for part of the Montgomery County railroad debt even though new bonds had been issued in a refunding. And in a previous case, the high tribunal upheld a provision in Robertson County's enabling statute which imposed an annual tax of $500 for four years on its citizens for their share of burdens assumed by parent Bracken County during the Civil War. Other settlements involved the partitioning of land. In 1842 the legislature provided that half of 6,000 acres given by the Commonwealth to Calloway County in 1834 should go to Marshall County, wholly created out of the former. Calloway County subsequently sold 3,920 acres for her own benefit and refused to transfer any of the remaining land to Marshall. The Court of Appeals ruled that Marshall County could recover at least half of the acreage unsold.[4]

To most critics, Kentucky's excessive number of counties meant that many were little better than paupers constituting a drain on more stable counties and the state treasury. In this context, a pauper county was one that received more state revenue than it produced. At first such a description fit counties mostly in eastern and southeastern Kentucky, but by 1890 it applied to nearly two-thirds of the state's counties. In marked contrast, the Bluegrass and urban counties of Fayette, Bourbon, Scott, Shelby, Woodford, Jefferson, Kenton, Campbell, and Mason paid 80 percent of the net revenue which went into the state treasury.[5]

Many observers saw a direct relationship between the number of Kentucky counties and county poverty. The abundance of counties with small populations meant there were often few qualified public officials, produced the need for more local juries, contributed to the state's high crime rate, and caused many regions to go without needed internal improvements. Shortages of competent county officials led to inadequate tax assessment and collection and incompetent fiscal management.

Vast numbers of small counties further meant that many were nothing more than "little centers from which radiate antagonisms" leading to feuds and other forms of violent crime necessitating continuous jury selection and criminal prosecution, the expense of which was largely borne by the state. Because government aid to transportation involved local government much more than state, an overabundance of small counties meant inadequate tax bases and lack of central planning. Residents of southeastern and eastern Kentucky themselves lamented that their county patterns made it more difficult to exploit the region's vast mineral and timber wealth because most counties had no funds to create efficient forms of transportation.[6]

Not every observer accepted the argument that local poverty and strains on the state treasury were caused by an overabundance of counties. Some noted that most of the state assistance to counties constituted funds for education which would be unaffected by the number of counties, while others argued that smaller counties rendered law enforcement and criminal prosecution more efficient rather than less. A few even advocated the creation of more counties as a means of more accessible justice, civil as well as criminal. But these voices were definitely in the minority. By 1890 most people favored a constitutional limitation on the number of new counties which could be created.[7]

Contests over the location of county seats within established counties closely resembled those over the creation of new counties. Although county seats were not usually moved in an established county, efforts to change those centers were not uncommon. Legislatures not infrequently let commissioners or even the voters determine county seat locations where new counties were being established, and in such cases conflicts could be intense. The commissioners appointed to establish Lee County were unable to agree on the location of a county seat and left the question to the voters, who supported the town of Beattyville over Proctor by a margin of nearly three to one.

Furious over defeat, Proctorites at first tried to secure the repeal of the statute creating Lee County and then unsuccessfully sought legislative removal of the seat of government to their community. On another occasion, the burning of the courthouse in Blandville occasioned an attempt by citizens in Wickliffe to become the Ballard County seat. After a heated campaign that involved alleged vote-buying and fraud, Wickliffe prevailed in a special election authorized by the legislature. Distraught Blandvillians challenged the outcome before the Court of Appeals, only to lose, even though it was proved that Wickliffe merchants had promised voters they would underwrite the cost of a new county courthouse. During the litigation, Ballard County's jail remained in Blandville while the new courthouse resided in Wickliffe.[8]

Kentuckians near a county border who were unhappy about residing in a particular county did not have to petition for the creation of a new county in order to gain relief; they could simply secure special legislation redrawing the county line. This happened at least two hundred times during the period of the third constitution and for a variety of reasons. Although almost always pleading that the seat of government in the next county was closer, petitioners for county-line changes sometimes actually desired to obtain lower tax rates or to run for office in their new counties. Usually such endeavors involved only a few acres and were successful, but occasionally proposed county-line redefinitions were more ambitious and sparked heated controversy. In 1877 the western border area around Knoxville in Pendleton County wanted to join Grant County on the pretense that most of its inhabitants worked in Williamstown, but Pendletonians resisted the attempt because too much territory would be lost (thirty-five square miles); they also claimed that the maneuver was simply a Republican gerrymander. In the end the effort failed.[9]

Sometimes county-line changes seemingly minor in nature became major alterations upon closer inspection and plunged neighboring counties into prolonged and bitter litigation. In

1890 the legislature redefined the boundary between Estill and Powell counties ostensibly because of uncertainty as to the proper line. When new surveys revealed that the redefinition had transferred 160 voters and taxable property worth $175,000 to Powell County, Estill County officials declared the statute invalid because of fraud and attempted to collect taxes from residents in the disputed territory. Faced with the prospect of double taxation, the residents successfully challenged Estill County's right to tax, the Court of Appeals refusing to look behind the statute for evidence of fraud. A similar dispute occurred between Shelby and Oldham counties in 1852. After the legislature transferred part of Shelby County to Oldham, officials of the former claimed it was impossible to establish the new county line from the statutory description and continued to assess residents in the affected area. In upholding the boundary alteration, the Court of Appeals ruled that vague statutory language and the failure to designate who should fix the new line did not render the legislation invalid.[10]

The presence of large numbers of so-called pauper counties, plus the added aggravation of county-seat and county-line disputes, prompted some critics to call for the abolition of certain numbers of counties. Seldom did such proposals reach the legislature and when they did, they usually languished in committee. But on one occasion the General Assembly seriously considered the question of abolition and very nearly agreed to such a proposition. In 1888 the General Assembly only narrowly defeated an effort to abolish Rowan County after a bloody feud had reduced the citizens of the area to near anarchy. Cynics suggested that the prospect of undermining Fleming County's Democratic posture by adding to it a Republican part of Rowan County influenced the Democratic legislature as much as the question of law and order.[11]

Most of the calls for consolidation of counties came from newspapers. In 1871 the *Maysville Bulletin* published one of the most searching analyses of the problem, calling for the abolition of all counties created since 1845 or at the least a permanent stop to the creation of new counties. In many of the smaller counties, the newspaper submitted, there were too few intelligent and competent men to run local affairs and government was "a ridiculous farce" with record-keeping "a muddle." In one instance, the paper reported, a healthy county with splendid turnpikes and bridges had given birth to several new counties whose smaller tax bases could not support macadamized roads and required state subsidy for routine expenditures. Five years later, the Lexington *Kentucky Gazette* offered still another formula for dealing with surplus counties. "Each and every county that has through a course of years proven itself incapable of supporting itself ought to be consolidated with another county," the *Gazette* boldly suggested, "and, if the new county still proves unable to take care of itself, let consolidation go on until they do become self sustaining."[12]

Even though county-abolition movements failed during the period of the third constitution, many people desired to incorporate restrictions against the creation of new counties in the fourth constitution. Some delegates claimed that the vast majority of people favored such restrictions, as well as some reduction in the number of counties, while others denied this, asserting that many localities were looking forward to the time when they could form themselves into new counties. While most legislators during the debates over the proposed abolition of Rowan County had presumed the right of the General Assembly to abolish a county, delegates to the constitutional convention three years later sharply divided over the question. Despite the virtual unanimity of opinion from such scholars as Thomas McIntyre Cooley, Joseph Story, and John F. Dillon that states could abolish their counties, surprising numbers of delegates argued to the contrary, evidence of the stature these local entities had attained during their first 100 years of existence. Some argued that whenever a legislature established a county and allowed its people to invest money in buildings, bridges, roads, and other capital assets, it implied a contract not to abolish it, a few even contending that the Dartmouth College case prevented abolition. One delegate went so far as to argue that counties had the same immunity from destruction as the states of the Union. Such argument failed to persuade a majority of delegates, who voted forty-eight to thirty-three to include a specific provision acknowledging the right of future legislatures to abolish counties. The convention overwhelmingly approved a general article prohibiting the creation of new counties of less than 400 square miles or whose proposed boundary line would run less than ten miles from a county seat.[13]

During the period of the third constitution, as before, counties did not perform duties not clearly prescribed by the constitution or statute without seeking legislative authorization or ratification. As the nineteenth century matured and society became more complex, the needs of county government and governors multiplied and the tendency to secure legislative authorization increased. By 1890, from 150 to 250 statutes of each legislative session normally concerned some aspect of county government.

County courts found it necessary to secure special legislation for a variety of matters. Bills were considered authorizing investment in internal improvements (usually conditioned upon voter approval), levying special taxes for the construction of buildings and other capital improvements, adopting special road laws, permitting claims payments not authorized under general laws, or selling public buildings such as poorhouses. Normally, too, the local tribunals needed to secure legislative ratification of delinquent levies, appointments to office made without quorums, questionable subscriptions to various internal improvement projects, and orders, judgments, and minutes not regularly read or signed. Miscellaneous statutes included permission to individual counties to establish additional magisterial districts or voting places.

County officers secured a wide variety of measures granting special jurisdiction. By virtue of such legislation the judge of the Boone County Court had jurisdiction after 1879 to try all complaints against surveyors of public roads; Madison's county judge was permitted after 1877 to practice law in any case involving the settlement of an estate when the fiduciary had not settled his accounts in the Madison County Court; the judges of the county courts of Warren, Scott, and Pendleton counties, if lawyers, were permitted to form partnerships with licensed lawyers to practice law in any court except their own; the judge of the Butler County Court was exempted from the general prohibition of county judges from bringing suits to settle the estates of deceased persons; and the county judges as presiding judges of the county quarterly courts were given a wide variety of jurisdictional limitations ranging from $100 to $500.[14]

Many of the statutes affecting justices of the peace constituted special legislation because they applied to the magistrates in certain counties only; this was especially true of legislation establishing limits to civil jurisdiction. Other special laws concerning county officers included those requiring certain county court clerks to index and cross-index their records, requiring certain officers to purchase certain books, benefiting certain officers such as sheriffs and constables by (for example) extending the time periods in which to collect fee bills and granting certain officers special powers.

The tendency of the legislature to exempt counties from the operation of general laws drew criticism from newspapers and other commentators. The *Maysville Bulletin* branded the practice "an evil one" and cited laws regulating the jurisdiction of justices of the peace as particularly offensive. "The justices in one half of the counties have jurisdiction in civil causes to the amount of fifty dollars, while in the other half they have jurisdiction to the amount of one hundred." Submitting that "uniformity in the operation of general laws is a fundamental requirement of good government," the paper derisively noted that county lines sometimes ran through the centers of towns, resulting in justices at one end of town having double the jurisdiction as those on the other end.[15]

The General Assembly's preoccupation with the special needs

of individual counties constituted only part of the general problem of local legislation which by 1860 had grown to be a dilemma for practically every state in the Union. More and more the nation's legislatures found themselves bogged down in trivia, passing laws for the benefit of the keepers of stud horses, jacks, and bulls; incorporating village graveyards; chartering numerous businesses; and changing the names of small towns (e.g., Buzzard's Roost to Upper Blue Lick Springs). The pernicious effects of such a system were obvious to many Kentuckians and applied as well to the legislative processes of other states. Describing the evils of special legislation generally as "vicious," "fraudulent," and "outrageous," observers noted more particularly that Kentucky's General Assembly had little time to cope with the general problems of the Commonwealth. When the legislators tended to such problems they often did so hastily and sloppily. So scandalous had the situation become that in 1879 politician-lawyer Robert M. Bradley was able to pen a satire of the whole legislative process, *A Sketch of Granny Short's Barbecue and the General Statutes of Kentucky*. Typical of their incongruity, Bradley observed, were statutes requiring commonwealth attorneys to prosecute all crimes within their districts, but forbidding them to practice law there except in civil proceedings. Such a "gross absurdity" in the statutes illustrated the tendency of Kentucky's legislators to be much better at politicking than at lawmaking. According to Bradley, even the ablest members of the bar were "at a loss how to advise their clients owing to the ambiguous" nature of legislation.[16]

While some argued that local legislation increased the power of the legislature over the counties, the reverse was often true. Legislators were so besieged with demands for local and special statutes that they sometimes lacked time to draft the necessary bills and had to rely on their petitioners to present their own drafts. County officers were no exception and county court order books contain resolutions authorizing the drafting of bills to achieve some special object of local government.

Nor was this process very democratic. A delegate to the

constitutional convention of 1890-1891 observed that whenever Kentucky's county residents met in local conventions they discussed national not local problems. In contrast, northerners, who relied more heavily on the township and town meetings, concentrated on local business. Often unafraid or unaware of local public opinion (internal improvement questions were an exception) and desirous of avoiding protracted discussions on the local level, county officials frequently bypassed their constituents and dealt directly with the county's legislative representatives. The local representative, usually unaware of significant sentiment opposing local propositions and acting in conjunction with the local state senator, secured most special legislation without debate or opposition by virtue of legislative courtesy, a presumption on the part of all legislators that "the man who represents a particular county legislates in all local matters for that county." What local legislators could not obtain by courtesy, they usually secured through vote-trading. Repeal of unpopular laws proved difficult, especially if a local representative or senator lived in an area remote from the locality affected by the statutes. Since county officers usually drafted the legislative bills affecting their own interests and since these bills were often routinely passed with little debate, the county officers in effect possessed de facto legislative powers made unique by their insulation from public scrutiny.

Because of the vast number of bills dealing with local matters (in 1873, 1,034 out of 1,119 statutes were local or special in nature) and because most legislators feared the wrath of special interests if they did not tend to their needs, the General Assembly inevitably put off to the end of the session proposals dealing with the Commonwealth's general needs. Consequently the solons passed few general laws, many of which were poorly drafted and ill considered. Kentucky's legislature had become in many respects nothing more than a codifier for special and local interests. All of this further enhanced the position of the counties in the state constitution.[17]

As the amount of local legislation increased, so did demands for its curtailment, if not abolition. Newspaper editors, legislators, and even some governors recommended a variety of solutions, including transferral of much of the business of local legislating to the county courts and the passage of a general law of incorporation. Before 1890 efforts at effective reform failed. A bill to dispense in part with local and private legislation introduced in 1860 met with summary defeat and represented one of the very few times legislators tried to grapple with the problem. During the Civil War, the General Assembly, doubtless because of the prevailing mood of crisis, resolved on more than one occasion to dispense completely with local legislation or to devote only specified periods of time to consideration of same, but attempts to follow these healthy precedents following the military conflict failed. On three postbellum occasions, Governor John Whyte Stevenson successfully vetoed local legislation dealing with counties, representing the only examples of such vetoes during the period of the third constitution. In 1869 he vetoed an act that would increase the power and jurisdiction of the constable of the first district in Larue County on the grounds that the statute in effect gave the county two sheriffs instead of one and would reduce the fees of the sheriff *de jure*, that the statute discriminated against other constables, and that acquiescence in such a law would permit some future legislature to abolish the sheriffalty, a constitutionally protected office. In the same year, Stevenson vetoed an act to exempt Livingston County from the provisions of a statute to prohibit county judges from bringing suits to settle the estates of deceased persons. Citing Article XIII, section 1, of the Constitution of 1850, the governor reasoned that the law violated the prohibition against "special, exclusive privileges or immunities" not in consideration of public service and the necessity for laws regulating the administration of justice in the respective counties to be uniform and equal in their operation. Finally in 1871 Stevenson vetoed legislation making it easier for Mercer countians to rectify errors in proceedings authorizing the sale of orphans' real estate, again on the grounds that laws should be general and not affect just one county. But apparently other governors of the period did not share Stevenson's concern for uniformity or feared to express such reservations in the form of vetoes, since no other governor in the period issued similar vetoes.[18]

By the eve of the constitutional convention of 1890-1891, many claimed that public outcries against local legislation had reached substantial proportions. In the convention itself some delegates asserted that virtually all Kentuckians demanded the abolition of local legislation and several introduced resolutions and amendments to that effect. A majority of delegates feared that a more general invalidation of special and local legislation could be evaded by subsequent legislatures and demanded prohibition of specific categories. In the end the convention outlawed a variety of local and special legislation, including statutes ratifying invalid or unauthorized acts of governmental officials or institutions, extending the period of lawful fee collection, authorizing the appointment of deputies, or locating or changing county seats. The convention also made uniform the jurisdiction of county judges, quarterly courts, and justices of the peace. Supporters of the reform asserted that they had eliminated at least nine-tenths of local and special legislation, and their claims seemed to ring true as the legislature began operating under the new constitution. The legislators devoted most of their time to general legislation, and the bound "Acts of the Legislature" were thereafter much slimmer volumes, containing very little local or special legislation.[19]

If counties enjoyed a one-sided relationship with the legislature, obtaining most of the local legislation they desired and enduring only minimal regulation, they maintained a more balanced association with towns and cities, requiring them to engage in more genuine negotiation. Especially in the area of politics, county residents sometimes complained about the outcome of such negotiations.

Political rivalry over the residence of party nominees occasionally plagued the relationship between county and city. In

July 1869 Fayette County Democrats accused city politicians and "flunkies" of establishing "superior claims of the city for every office worth having," thereby making Lexington "odious to the county round about it." Submitting that the city was much more dependent upon the county than the county upon the city, county interests accused the city of dominating most of the important county offices since 1862. City spokesmen denied they monopolized county offices, pointing out that the countians had possessed the lion's share of the spoils until 1862 and that afterwards many of the party nominees had resided in the county before being elected and moving to the city. The debate raged into the next year with countians demanding half of the nominations and city Democrats urging an end to intraparty conflict so that full attention could be given to defeating "Black Republicans."[20]

City-county tensions over the residence of Democratic nominees simmered throughout the next two decades. The party's convention of March 1874 was particularly stormy with county delegates threatening to boycott the party ticket if a county resident was not nominated for county judge. The threat apparently worked as the party nominated John T. Stevenson, who lived outside of Lexington. At the convention of April 1878 county delegates renewed their demands for a fair share of party nominees and some even suggested that if enough qualified candidates were available, the county should secure all the nominations, since the city had its own government. Seven years later while initially denying a rivalry between town and county over county offices, the *Lexington Weekly Press* contradicted itself by endorsing the view that most, if not all, of these officers should reside in the county.[21]

It must, however, be noted that the urban-rural conflict which marred relations within Fayette County did not represent a general condition throughout the state. In most cases county residents and their governments enjoyed harmonious relations with their urban neighbors. Jefferson County and Louisville took care to secure elaborate statutory protection against conflict. Both Louisville and the Jefferson County Court enjoyed virtual autonomy over its own affairs within its own boundaries. A statute of 1860 provided in part that only justices of the peace residing outside of the city could vote on the county levy court (similar to the court of claims in other counties), although a subsequent statute did allow Louisville justices to vote for county officers elected by the court. But the two governments could not operate in complete isolation from one another, and when they did jointly incur expenses or participate together in planning, they divided responsibilities and financial obligations by written agreement or according to statutory formula. The city paid the larger share of the county judge's salary, eleven-sixteenths according to statutory prescription.[22]

Statutes dealing with county-city affairs provided also that each government could sue the other over outstanding claims, but litigation between the two was rare. Probably the most serious dispute between the governments arose in 1867-1868 over a proposition by the county to build a new jail. County authorities were anxious for the city to share the expense of construction, as well as the responsibility for maintaining the new structure. Finding it impossible to agree with the city on a formula of construction cost allocation, the levy court proceeded to initiate plans for construction of a new jail on its own and threatened to secure legislative authority to tax city residents for their share of the cost. Faced with such determination and the probability that the county tax might exaggerate the city's "fair share," city authorities finally entered into a formal agreement with the county dividing costs and responsibilities, a contract formally codified by the General Assembly. By its terms the city and county allocated construction and maintenance costs according to the proportionate numbers of white tithables within each governmental unit. Despite a rumor that dissidents within the city, apparently displeased with the city's assumption of over three-fourths of the expense, were endeavoring to stall construction, the building of the jail proceeded on schedule, each government appointing commissioners to oversee the construction.[23]

Most of the other urban counties of nineteenth-century Kentucky maintained harmony with the cities within their boundaries. In part this tranquillity resulted from far-sighted county and city officials seeking local legislation accommodating the needs of the cities. Although neither Covington nor Newport was a county seat, each benefited from a series of statutes requiring county services, including courts, to be offered in each on a monthly basis. Legislation also provided that each city would pay its share of the expense of court sittings and other county services.[24]

Even potentially contentious problems of urban annexation of surrounding county territory proved amenable to generally easy solution. For example, a statute secured by local authorities in 1867 provided that the city of Louisville had to pay the county "a fair and just portion, pro rata, of the existing debt or debts of said county to the extent of the taxes or means of the county being reduced or diminished by the extension of said city boundaries beyond the present taxable limits of said city." The statute further provided that county lands annexed into the city would not be liable for city taxes until they were given streets. Numerous annexations by Newport of surrounding Campbell County land produced few, if any, ostensible conflicts. In an era when cities and towns were growing rapidly even in predominately agricultural Kentucky, annexation was often long overdue. The lament of the *Lexington Leader* in July 1890 that over 750 Fayette countians enjoyed all the benefits of city life without paying its taxes probably typified the situation of many Kentuckians who lived adjacent to cities.[25]

Aside from rivalries over court days and railroads, counties generally enjoyed favorable relations with one another during the period of the third constitution. Inevitably conflicts arose over probate jurisdiction, but these occurred infrequently and

LITTLE KINGDOMS   17

were resolved by the Court of Appeals or the General Assembly. The legislature determined by statute in 1869 that jurisdiction over the estate of Joseph F. Wilson should reside in the Hancock County Court even though the Marshall County Court was asserting its own claim in the Hancock Circuit Court. Occasionally, too, disputes erupted between counties over proposed bridges, but again the legislature and courts usually resolved the issues without undue controversy. By statute it was provided that when two counties could not agree upon the necessity of building a bridge between the two, the appropriate circuit court should resolve the issue. In 1874, for instance, the Boyle County Circuit Court upheld its county's contention that a bridge between it and Garrard County was not necessary because two already existed and Boyle County's debt would not permit further borrowings; and in 1886 the Court of Appeals reversed a Grayson Circuit Court and ruled that a bridge between Grayson and Breckinridge counties was not indispensable and would seriously imperil Grayson County's financial stability.[26]

The preoccupation of the General Assembly with the needs of individual counties reinforced their semi-autonomous nature. Although theoretically supervising the counties, the legislature was in reality surrendering much of its constitutional control by immersing itself in the processes of local legislation. Because county officials initiated most of the bills which became local legislation, because the local legislator generally obtained what he wanted, and because the legislature had no time to consider each piece of legislation with sufficient thoroughness, the counties were in many ways legislating for themselves and exercising a kind of home rule. Harmony between counties and their neighboring cities and towns and the creation of fewer counties after 1850 did not detract from these characteristics of independence and sovereignty.

2.
LITTLE KINGS

As with all institutions, the usefulness of county governments in nineteenth-century Kentucky depended upon the competence of their officers. Alleging that many county officers performed inadequately, mid-nineteenth-century reformers adopted a simple remedy: they prescribed heavy doses of democracy, providing that the voters would elect most county officials. But they and subsequent legislators failed to alter the basic structure of local government and the fundamental responsibilities of most officials. It remained to be seen whether democracy alone could alter the nature and problems of the local constitution.

The reformers of 1849-1850 sought to redress the cumbersomeness of the old county court system by consolidating much of the judicial power of the county court in a single officer of county government, the county judge. Although the office was not without its problems, it may be said that the drafters of the Constitution of 1850 were in large part successful in their attempts to bring a form of unitary judicial leadership to the often directionless county judiciary of antebellum Kentucky. Given almost exclusive control over county probate and fiduciary matters, the county judge also served as the presiding officer of the county court of claims and himself usually constituted the quarterly court, possessed of important civil and criminal jurisdiction. The county judge also had licensing and naturalization powers, both of which sometimes produced controversy. Nonetheless the county judge was in no sense the chief executive officer of the county, with supervisory powers over other county officers and county business as a whole. In most instances, each county official was responsible only to the state and to a collection of statutes, though just as often this responsibility was vague and remote. In short, except in judicial matters, county government during the period of the third constitution was headless.

The legislature originally gave to the county judges as the judicial officers of the quarterly courts power to hear civil cases involving the recovery of money or personalty of up to $100 in value. This amount was later increased to $200 for many counties and as high as $500 for a few. Such jurisdiction was in part concurrent with that of the circuit courts and that of justices of the peace who initially could hear cases involving money or other personalty in value up to $50 (later increased for some as high as $250). Apparently the judges enjoyed full quarterly court dockets in most counties until the legislature in the mid-1870s increased the jurisdiction of many justices of the peace and created more courts of common pleas, both of which encroached rather substantially on the business of the quarterly courts and rendered some of their sessions almost useless.[1]

The county judge also was a conservator of the peace, could entertain actions against constables for defalcation in office, grant injunctions, hold inquests upon idiots and lunatics, perform marriages, appoint inspectors of illuminating oils, and had appellate jurisdiction over certain of the civil cases of the justices of the peace and police judges. In addition, the county judges shared important criminal jurisdiction with the justices of the peace, including the power to hold examining courts in cases of alleged felonies (their powers over alleged homicides being exclusive after 1884) and the power to hear cases involving riots, routs, or breaches of the peace. In 1876 the judges were given jurisdiction concurrent with circuit and criminal courts over misdemeanors in an effort to relieve the crowded dockets of the latter two tribunals. County judges did not uniformly greet all this accretion of power with great joy. Some complained that they were overworked and underpaid, and others sought higher salaries and more assistance. Initially county judges had to be their own quarterly court clerks, but eventually they won the right to appoint separate clerks. Courts of claims sometimes eased the financial distress of judges by voting them higher salaries and in some counties, circuit court judges appointed them their special commissioners, one of the few governmental positions which they could hold simultaneously with their judgeships.[2]

Soon after the adoption and implementation of the Constitution of 1850, a correspondent to the *Frankfort Commonwealth*, emphasizing the seriousness and complexity of the newly created county judge's probate and fiduciary responsibilities and the need for patience and expertise to execute them properly, cautioned voters not to "sustain any individual for county judge unless he could cheerfully commit his estate to his hands after his death, and the rights of his tender children." If we can believe the testimony of another interested observer, that of J. Fletcher Johnston, candidate for Fayette county judge in 1878, some voters did not adhere to the *Commonwealth*'s caveat. Johnston alleged that county judges were too often remiss in their probate and fiduciary duties. Many of them permitted irresponsible executors, administrators, and guardians to squander the assets of helpless widows and orphans. Others permitted settlements of estates without sufficient accounting and examination. Some activity of county judges in this area bordered on criminality. "To tell what I actually know in this connection would startle the people and set them firmly in the resolve to protect interest by selecting competent and faithful men for places of trust," he added. Claiming that conversations with a former county judge of a neighboring county reinforced his impressions, Johnston argued that the solution to the problem lay not in sweeping reforms but in greater vigilance by the voters.[3]

Yet criticisms such as Johnston's were not widespread, and during the period of the third constitution reformers did little to alter the basic structure of probate and fiduciary administration. The General Assembly did provide for a public administrator and guardian in each county, but he had jurisdiction only when court-appointed fiduciaries failed to qualify. Likewise the county judge always had the power to appoint a special commissioner to make settlements with fiduciaries, but this power was discretionary. Nor did the delegates at the constitutional convention of 1890-1891 seriously consider the creation of separate probate courts any more than their counterparts had done so some forty-one years earlier. Aggrieved widows and orphans largely had to rely on the circuit courts to redress the errors of county judges, an expensive, time-consuming, and often unrewarding experience. Some courts did rule against county judges in flagrant cases, but this was not a common occurrence.[4]

Observers noted that if county judges did not always command the legal expertise needed for effective probate and fiduciary administration, they more often exhibited the responsibility necessary for efficient management of the county's fiscal affairs. This was especially true in the area of appropriations where county judges not infrequently resisted efforts of courts of claims to invest unwisely in shaky railroad ventures; some went so far as to refuse to issue bonds already supported by a majority of voters. A forceful county judge could work his will against a recalcitrant court of claims even though he was allowed to vote on appropriations only in case of a tie. In one reported incident, Benjamin F. Graves, Fayette county judge, threatened to seize the county attorney and the assembled justices of the peace by the napes of their necks if they did not vote in accordance with his wishes. On this occasion and many others, Graves triumphed in stormy struggles over control of local fiscal policy.[5]

County judges had virtually complete discretion in the granting of liquor licenses in the county and posed in a sense as overseers of popular morality. The Harrison county judge, for example, once refused to grant a tavern license in one locale because, in his opinion, its residents were "too free and unbridled" in their use of whiskey; and on one occasion, the

Rockcastle county judge refused to grant any liquor licenses in his county. The Court of Appeals more than once supported such broad exercises of power. Following the Civil War, county voters assumed more control over the administration of liquor laws by successfully petitioning the legislature for the right to vote on local option laws which, if approved, prohibited the sale of liquor in all or parts of counties.[6]

During the nativist controversy in the 1850s, arguments arose over whether county judges had the power to naturalize aliens. Nativists generally claimed they did not (especially in Democratic counties), pointing to a federal statute requiring naturalizing courts to have common law jurisdiction and arguing that county courts lacked such power. Supporters pointed out that county courts did have limited common law powers as, for example, in the partitioning of land. The Court of Appeals decided that city courts had jurisdiction, and although it never ruled on the rights of county courts, these tribunals were reported exercising such power long after the nativistic controversy had abated.[7]

Appraisals of county judges during the period of the third constitution were mixed. Early in the period, "A Farmer," writing in a Frankfort newspaper, denigrated the jurists, beseeching the General Assembly to devise a plan to "command better qualified county judges" and arguing that "in many of the counties the office is filled by clever men, but totally incompetent to discharge the vast and important duties entrusted to them." Periodically throughout the era observers complained about the allegedly debilitating effects of the elective judiciary without singling out county judges for any special condemnation. Occasionally critics leveled charges at individual county judges. The editor of the *Stanford Interior Journal*, for example, accused the newly elected county judge of Lincoln County of locking him in his office and threatening to beat him unless he retracted an unfavorable editorial.[8]

On the other hand, there were many individual notices of other county judges which were more complimentary. The

Lexington *Kentucky Gazette* observed that Fayette County's newly elected county judge, W. B. Kinkead, "appears perfectly at home on the bench, and pushes all business through that comes before him with commendable alacrity. He is most certainly the right man in the right place." The *Gazette* likewise praised Kinkead's predecessor as a "widely known and highly respected" judge, while a decade later the *Lexington Leader* described incumbent judge P. P. Johnston as "one of our purest public men, fair and impartial in the administration of his high office." The *Maysville Bulletin* labeled two of Mason County's postwar judges as exemplary, while observers in Franklin, Bourbon, and Laurel counties were known to speak approvingly of other judges, sprinkling their characterizations with such terms as "venerable," "honored landmarks," and "dignity."[9]

Perhaps the best example of the nineteenth-century Kentucky county judge is Benjamin F. Graves, who presided over the Fayette County Court for more than fifteen years. Failing at several business ventures before studying law, Graves became a justice of the peace at the age of forty and shortly thereafter, in 1851, the first county judge of Fayette County. Often crude (once seizing a young bride he had just married and forcing a kiss upon her startled face), exhibiting only a superficial knowledge of the law ("some of his decisions, if put in print, might be calculated to produce a laugh"), and tending to fall asleep on the bench (when once awakened by counsel, he protested that "this court can hear just as well when it's asleep as when it's awake"), he nonetheless earned the respect of most of his contemporaries with the intrinsic fairness of his decisions. Favoring equity over the law and manifesting a strong common sense, his decisions were seldom reversed by higher tribunals. Other county judges were equally as colorful and some very enterprising. The judge of the Kenton County Court specialized in marrying minors from other counties and protected his flourishing business by refusing to grant licenses to justices of the peace or ministers to compete against him. A certain Judge Smith of the Bullitt County Court, when accused of favoritism by an attorney, adjourned court, administered a sound thrashing to the sarcastic counsel, voluntarily appeared before a justice of the peace to be fined twenty-five dollars for disorderly conduct, returned to the bench, and continued the trial.[10]

While some doubted the competence of individual judges and others marveled at their eccentricity, few denied the importance of the office. Many pronounced it the most significant position in the local constitution, its powers most profoundly affecting the greatest numbers of people, demanding the skills of a lawyer, accountant, and businessman. And most seemed to acquiesce (however reluctantly) in the appraisal of a delegate to the constitutional convention of 1890-1891 who declared that "the county judgeship is so engrafted upon the affections of the people, so deeply in their prejudices in favor of it, that it would be dangerous to abolish the county judge."[11]

If the county judge was the most powerful county officer, the sheriff was a close second. Possessed of those responsibilities which he had retained almost from the beginning of the Commonwealth, the sheriff was the principal tax collector of the county, its chief election and law enforcement officer, and the primary executive officer of the circuit, criminal, and common pleas courts. In the latter capacity he summoned jurors, served processes, and enforced judgments. He also sometimes acted as a court-appointed estate administrator.

Although the sheriff received a commission on the county levy and state taxes which he collected, his responsibilities to do so were more often a source of frustration than of profit. Statutory insufficiencies probably accounted for most of the sheriff's frustrations, which were born of the fact that in a vast majority of counties nearly 20 percent of the taxpayers were routinely turned in as delinquent, rendering it more difficult for the sheriff to make a final accounting. As the sheriff of Franklin County complained to the state auditor in March 1872, it was cheaper for taxpayers to pay delinquency fines of only 5 percent of the tax due than to borrow money at the going rate of 10 percent. Furthermore, sheriffs were forced to ride from precinct to precinct and sometimes from house to house collecting from each taxpayer.[12]

The legislative journals and statute books are filled with special bills and acts granting individual sheriffs more time in which to collect delinquent taxes, while the county court order books were likewise replete with the entries of the settlements by ex-sheriffs of delinquent taxes due (sometimes for more than ten years). Each year the state auditor squabbled with more than a few sheriffs about taxes for which there was no accounting. In many counties the problem of back taxes was so great and the amount owed so large that special collectors were appointed and, in a few, back tax lists were sold to the highest bidder. Often counties never did collect back taxes from sheriffs, and courts of claims proceedings were occasionally the scenes of heated controversy between sheriffs and other county officials over the question. So great was the resistance of some sheriffs to the duty of tax collection that the legislature felt compelled to pass a statute imposing a stiff fine on all of those who failed to execute their revenue bonds, although an earlier statute provided for forfeiture of office in such event. In 1878 Governor James B. McCreary vetoed a bill which would have exempted the sheriffs of four counties from the forfeiture statute on the grounds that it would encourage the sheriffs of almost every other county to do likewise and result "in the greater part of the state revenue remaining uncollected." Unusual indeed was the statute passed in 1863 to release the former sheriff of Lyon County from tax delinquency liability because it appeared that "such failure was the result of his misfortune and not of any culpable neglect of duty." Rare also was the elaborately contrived but unsuccessful attempt of the sheriff of Jessamine County to defraud the county of taxes already collected. Some sheriffs obtained partial relief from what was often a burden by securing from the General Assembly special statutes relieving them of the task of collecting railroad taxes. Particularly painful to many sheriffs was the discovery in 1863 that Thomas A. Page, state auditor of accounts from 1850 to 1861, had embezzled "large amounts of the public revenue" and that they who had collected same would probably be liable for the deficiencies.[13]

Not surprisingly these deficiencies produced periodic calls for reform. In February 1871 "quite a number of sheriffs" met in Frankfort to discuss ways to secure speedier collection of taxes. A correspondent to the *London Mountain Echo* called for the abolition of the "antiquated" obligation of sheriffs to ride around the county collecting taxes and for the establishment of a central tax-collecting office such as that which existed in all of the "progressive states." To the distress of most sheriffs and other reformers, none of these efforts was successful.[14]

The sheriff's constant involvement in the daily process of executing civil judgments and criminal warrants made him financially vulnerable in other ways. For example, the Court of Appeals ruled on separate occasions that sheriffs were liable for failure to return an execution without cause, for negligently failing to arrest a person named in a warrant, for willfully taking insufficient security from those arrested for unlawful gaming, for false returns of deputies upon execution on an estate, and for mistakenly selling property thought to have belonged to a debtor but actually belonging to a third party. But more to the point, such activity rendered more insecure the financial position of the sheriff's sureties, both on his bond to guarantee faithful performance of his general duties and his bonds to insure lawful execution of his tax-collecting functions. The digests are full of cases involving the liability of the sureties of misfeasant sheriffs and the statute books of acts granting special relief to some of these sureties in distress.[15]

For all this potential grief, sheriffs in most counties received very little income from their official duties. During most of the period their commission on tax collections represented, in the words of the state auditor, "a mere pittance," and by 1875 the master commissioners were making serious inroads on their fees from civil cases. So critical had the problem become that more than a few sheriffs resigned or refused to qualify. In 1878 the legislature authorized the auditor to appoint special tax collectors in counties without sheriffs and to permit the collectors to reserve a commission much larger than that awarded sheriffs. This statute only aggravated the dilemma by prompting still more sheriffs to resign their offices and arrange for friends to be appointed special collectors under whom they served as deputies in order to secure increased compensation. In an effort at partial remedy, the legislature in 1882 implemented a suggestion of the state auditor that sheriffs be given larger commissions for tax collections.[16]

Yet in the larger, more prosperous counties where the office could return a handsome profit, politicians continued to seek the sheriffalty eagerly and resourcefully. Frequently political parties held primaries solely to nominate for the sheriffalty and competition at those times, as well as in the general election, was usually keen. Many candidates advertised their choices for deputies or at least promised they would appoint respectable men from all parts of the county. In some primaries, voters actually nominated deputies and in at least one general election voters elected them, although usually the sheriff himself appointed his assistants.[17]

Clearly a prospective sheriff's announced choices as his deputy-designates could be crucial in close elections. William M. Chinn reportedly won the Democratic nomination for sheriff in Franklin County in 1872 because voters understood that his brother Franklin would be his deputy. And voters in some counties doubtlessly realized that chief-deputy designates would actually become the sheriff-in-fact or that the deputies collectively would divide the responsibilities and profits of the office equally. Such practices were rather commonplace and represented ways in which a man or men in a sheriff's office evaded the constitutional requirement that a sheriff serve for only two consecutive two-year terms. Sometimes an individual, designating himself as the chief deputy, announced another as the candidate for sheriff but upon winning the office actually controlled its responsibilities, profits, and patronage. In other instances, groups of deputies took turns as candidates for sheriff and, after securing election, reappointed one another as deputies. In either case, such tactics usually insured the perpetuation of the incumbency. To enhance the prospects of victory, the establishment sometimes wooed or intimidated voters by extending the time for payment of taxes or executions, or by threatening the prompt implementation of a potentially embarrassing legal action.[18]

With all its negative features, chiefly resulting from the unpleasantries of tax-collection, the sheriffalty continued in the second half of the nineteenth century to be a position of power and significance. Some even rated it above the county judgeship, since the sheriff had more personal contact with greater numbers of people. William B. Allen devoted an entire chapter in his *Kentucky Officer's Guide and Legal Hand-Book* to "the office of sheriff" because of its "great importance, trust, and authority." Largely because of its crucial position in the election process, party leaders, especially in closely contested counties, emphasized the need to secure the sheriffalty. J. F. Robinson, Jr., chairman of the Fayette Democratic Committee, warned his fellow party-members in 1876 that to lose the sheriffalty would surrender his county "to the evils of Radical rule." It was the best and worst of jobs.[19]

Once an office comparable to the sheriffalty in prestige, the justice of the peace somewhat receded in power and stature during the second half of the nineteenth century. No longer collectively comprising the county court, the justices still constituted the court of claims and retained most of their multifarious judicial duties. As the lowest tier in the Commonwealth's judicial system, the justices heard petty civil and criminal cases, were an examining court for felony charges, maintained jurisdiction over riots and disorderly conduct, and enforced numerous statutes, including those prohibiting illegal peddling, disturbance of public worship, and gambling. In most counties they held court four times a year for as long as it took to dispose of all pending business.[20]

LITTLE KINGS   29

One of the major complaints of the reformers at the constitutional convention of 1849-1850 was that there were too many justices of the peace in the Commonwealth, observers estimating that there were approximately 1,500 for Kentucky's 100 counties. Although many delegates bemoaned the excess of county magistrates, they did not limit their number and left that question to future legislatures. The first legislature meeting under the new constitution reduced the number of justices of the peace by over 300, but subsequent legislatures gradually increased the number so that by 1889 there were approximately 2,000 local jurists. While there were 119 counties in that year, still the average per county was nearly seventeen, representing an increase of nearly two per county since 1850.[21]

Despite the ability of the justices collectively to formulate county fiscal policy and make decisions on local investments in internal improvements, generally neither voters nor politicians manifested much interest in the office. Occasionally county party leaders would launch a spirited and well-organized drive to capture control of the board of magistrates. This occurred in Franklin County in 1859 when Democrats ousted the American party's majority control of that board. More typical was the election in Nelson County in 1852 in which P. C. Slaughter was elected a magistrate "without any solicitation on his part" after his only opponent withdrew as soon as he learned people were voting for him. Periodically, newspaper editors chided the electorate for ignoring magisterial elections, claiming the offices were much more important than commonly supposed. Such apathy doubtless resulted in part from the poor pay of justices and contributed to the rather large number of justices of the peace who resigned their positions during the course of a year. By statute the governor temporarily filled vacancies until the next regular election, and in making such appointments he usually relied heavily on the advice of the county judge, the other justices of the peace, and any other county officers who happened to make recommendations.[22]

During almost every legislative session until 1874, certain

legislators attempted to increase the civil jurisdiction of the justices of the peace to include money and personalty controversies involving up to $100 in value. In 1874, such a statute was enacted, but it applied to only fifty counties. Such moves usually touched off debate about the relative worth of the justices. Proponents of an increased jurisdiction argued that most magistrates were honest and fair judges, bringing quick solutions to many of the problems of their constituents without undue expense or insistence upon complex pleadings. Claiming to speak in behalf of the "horny-handed yeomanry of the county," Representative J. W. Ogilvie argued in April 1873 that the masses benefited from such cheap justice and defended the justices against charges of incompetence. Ogilvie maintained that "a large majority of justices [were] men of splendid practical ability," who, although they might lack education and legal training, were "decidedly superior" to members of the higher judiciary "in practical common sense, in virtue, and in a desire to administer justice in its Christian purity." The common man, Ogilvie and others submitted, deserved an inexpensive and simple form of justice and should not be dependent upon the costly, time-consuming, and often complex proceedings of higher tribunals.[23]

Others held similar opinions about the justices of the peace as is evident from contemporary appraisals of individual magistrates and collective assessments at the constitutional convention of 1890-1891. Fayette County newspapers uniformly praised their county magistrates as typified by the *Weekly Press*'s estimation that a newly elected justice would "doubtless preside with characteristic dignity and urbanity." Obituary notices revealed that throughout the Commonwealth certain counties had held particular justices in the highest esteem, as in the cases of the late "Squire Rutter" of Harrison County, who was eulogized as an "estimable man.... well and favorably known as an honest and upright man," and George W. Gwin of Franklin County, a justice for thirty years whose "entire course as a public officer has been characterized by honesty and impartiality.... never swerv[ing] from strict justice in the discharge of official duty." A delegate to the constitutional convention commented that "for the preservation of the peace, for the enforcement of law and order, for the elevation of the morals of the communities in which they have presided, they have accomplished more than any other class of men in this broad land."[24]

Opponents of increased magisterial jurisdiction, as well as critics in general, found most of the magistrates to be incompetent. Shortly before the Civil War, a justice of the peace himself castigated his fellow magistrates on the poor quality of their record-keeping. Contending that "a quarto volume of one thousand pages would not afford space sufficient to record the blunders made by the magistrates of a single county in Kentucky," the justice of the peace argued that if a "good clerk" examined the record books of almost any fellow-magistrate he would "be struck with astonishment." The in-house critic submitted that the system of an elective judiciary certainly had done nothing to improve the quality of the local magistracy, a charge readily echoed by the *Paris Western Citizen* some thirteen years later. Reflecting the sentiments of most critics, certain delegates at the constitutional convention of 1890-1891 labeled the county magistracy as a "class of men whose judgment [did not] commend itself very largely to the respect of the people." Voters, they contended, were apathetic during the election campaigns of would-be justices because they were by and large insignificant men lacking common sense and good judgment. One delegate expressed more ominous beliefs, describing the local officers as "the most dangerous body in every county of the commonwealth," men without much property themselves who imposed taxes on others and paid very little themselves.[25]

On balance, detractors of the institution appear to have been more accurate in their assessment of the local magistracy. An anonymous writer for the *Courier-Journal* best summarized the realities of the position. "There are not a few justices that are really, as they were intended to be, learned in the law," he observed. "That such are in a minority," he added, was a necessary consequence of the "very small compensation that is paid to the incumbents of the office, except in a few populous localities." Because of the poor pay and the paucity of lawyers in many places, Kentuckians had come to expect that most justices would not be learned in the law. But they did expect that the magistrates would be men "of character, fair intelligence and good judgment." Those who did measure up to this standard were "extremely useful men in their districts, not only by giving intelligent decisions of small controversies that arise, but also by giving good advice by which many lawsuits are avoided." Ironically, by dignifying the office, the prestigious squires served ultimately to degrade it by making it attractive to inferior men. Because of the poor pay and time-consuming burdens, respected men too often shunned the office, leaving it to incompetents whose "ludicrous mistakes" made both themselves and their positions seem ridiculous.[26]

Observers often commented that not even God himself knew how a justice of the peace would decide a case. Decisions were sometimes incongruous and often humorous examples of fireside equity. A Kenton County magistrate in one instance reportedly fined a man for selling candy on Sunday, but dismissed a charge of selling beer because it was an essential commodity. A Franklin County squire, upon learning of the innocence of a man whom he had ordered whipped for horse-stealing, replied, "It's all right, the fellow needed the thrashing anyhow." Famous for their decisions which split the difference, a magistrate in Pendleton County ruled for both parties in a trespass suit. Flexibility, even ingenuity, characterized the decisions of the justice who dissolved a marriage so that the wife could testify against her husband in a wife-beating case and his colleague who married a couple only after forcing the bride to swear off other men.[27]

The conduct of other justices of the peace bordered on negligence, if not illegality. In 1872 the *Georgetown Weekly*

Times and the county attorney accused two Scott County magistrates of illegally admitting an accused murderer to bail, and three years earlier a Fayette County newspaper denounced two Woodford County magistrates for discriminating against black defendants. Critics chided Jefferson County squires for failing to return marriage certificates to the county clerk's office. Other reported allegations involved possible conflicts of interest, false imprisonment, wrongful discharge of debtors, illegal arraignment, and pervasive corruption.[28]

Although cynics could justifiably accuse many of Kentucky's justices of the peace of being incompetent, negligent, ludicrous, and even corrupt, they nonetheless underestimated the office by branding it too as inconsequential. The most perceptive critics understood that the local magistracy wielded potentially great power. Writing in 1873 in opposition to the imminent legislative increase of magisterial civil jurisdiction, "Green Bag" warned "if the proposed bill becomes a law, it will prove to Kentucky what the *coup d'etat* did to France." Claiming that the justices of the peace already had "immense leverage," the correspondent predicted that "nothing but a multitude of future Sedans" could rescue Kentuckians from the two would-be "imperial Louis Napoleons" which would reside in each justice's precinct. Already the local jurists exercised "absolute and unlimited sovereignty," in the opinion of the writer. Eschewing all written authority in their pursuit of "jesstiss" and "ekkity," most magistrates relied exclusively on their "Guides to Justices" and their own unique conception of the law. One lawyer when advised by a justice that his references to a learned commentator were to no avail, "explained apologetically that he had no purpose of changing his honor's opinion, but merely desired to show what a d---d fool Story was." Whether the justices of the peace were "anachronisms" and "absurdities" as some contended, or "institutions of the last importance and the bulwarks of social order" as others maintained, they were clearly masters of their own bailiwicks.[29]

The so-called democratic reforms of 1849-1850 produced

little impact on the realities of the office of county clerk. It was a position of great profit before 1850, and as such often sold to the highest bidder; it remained remarkably unchanged after mid-century. In Jefferson County alone, the post earned $10,000 or more annually and caused aspirants for the office to spend large sums in their campaigns, some of which was allegedly used to buy votes. The clerks of populous counties commanded much patronage, and armies of incumbent or would-be deputies earnestly canvassed for votes in every election. But in less populous counties, as before, the office earned very little, and occupants not infrequently served also as the local clerks of the circuit courts in order to make ends meet. Democracy also had little effect on the tendency of individual men and families to dominate the office for long periods of time. In Perry County, for example, Jesse Combs was the circuit and county court clerk from 1820 to 1873 and was succeeded by his grandson Ira J. Davidson.[30]

If the political realities of the county court clerkship changed little during the period of the third constitution, the responsibilities of the office did grow more complex as the economy of the Commonwealth matured. The clerk became not only a recorder of many kinds of legal documents but also an auditor of tax records and a compiler of statistics. So complicated were the clerk's duties that by the end of the Civil War groups of them were clamoring for legislative clarification of their statutory obligations. But the General Assembly did little more than periodically require the clerks to index better and to preserve their records in regular-sized books. The expertise needed to be a competent clerk usually meant that most began as deputies at a relatively young age, a practice officially recognized by the Court of Appeals when it ruled that it was valid for a deputy clerk who was a minor to take an acknowledgment and receipt of a deed.[31]

Some clerks who were also lawyers apparently still relied on the rather traditional practice of associating with other clerk-lawyers in an effort to bolster their income by taking advantage of the leverage afforded by their office. Although the legislature before 1850 had prohibited clerks from practicing law in their own courts, they were not prevented from practicing in other courts or from forming partnerships with other clerks until 1873, at which time they were prevented also from leasing part of their offices to a practicing attorney.[32]

Despite the increasing burdens of their office and their often low pay, there were few public complaints and little recorded litigation suggesting that the county court clerks of the period of the third constitution generally performed less than competently. The available evidence rather supports the observation of the editor of the Frankfort *Kentucky Yeoman*, who wrote in 1869 that he had recently corresponded with all the state's county clerks and discovered that they were "an educated class of citizens."[33]

The other officials of county government performed more in the manner of sheriffs and justices of the peace than county judges and clerks. While the county attorney was not a constitutional officer during the period of the first two constitutions, his stature and duties had grown so by 1850 that the authors of the third constitution included his office in the new frame of government. By statute he represented the county before the county courts and all other tribunals, advised the court and all county officers, screened all claims before the court of claims, and opposed what he regarded as improper petitions for tavern or merchants' licenses. He also prosecuted rioters and those who breached the peace, all felony charges before examining courts (after 1884 assisted the commonwealth attorney in the prosecution of felonies committed in his county), delinquent county taxpayers, attorneys in his counties wrongfully withholding judgments collected for clients, and nonresidents for failing to list their lands with the county clerk.[34]

As with most county officers, opinions differ as to the competence and importance of the county attorney. Some observers submitted that he was even more important than the commonwealth's attorney, since he not only was indispensable to the latter in the prosecution of major criminal cases (especially after 1884) but also was a principal legal figure within the structure of county government. Especially significant, they argued, was his ability to trim county expenses by paring down excessive claims before the fiscal court. On the other hand, detractors of the office submitted that it was difficult to find good county attorneys because of the poor pay. Supporters countered by noting that in most counties, the county attorney spent only about one-third of his time in his official capacity and the rest at private practice and could therefore earn an adequate living. On balance, the critics of the office appear to have been most accurate in their assessment, although on occasion individual county attorneys performed exceptionally well. Most county attorneys seem to have been ambitious young lawyers who desired to use the office to advance themselves professionally and politically, or older barristers who needed the salaries and fees to supplement their incomes. Whether old or young, successful candidates for the position apparently often allied themselves with powerful families. Their average annual income seldom exceeded $500, although attorneys for the most prosperous and populous counties made much more than that. And most of them lacked either the experience or the native intelligence to furnish their respective counties with first-rate legal expertise.[35]

The jailer earned much more money from his office than the county attorney, although he probably performed his duties no more efficiently. Generally regarded as the most lucrative position in county government, the jailer commanded a variety of fees from all levels of government for imprisoning, shackling, maintaining, and transporting state and federal prisoners. Also custodian of the public buildings in the public square, including the courthouse, clerk's offices, jail, and stray-pen, Kentucky's 119 jailers earned an estimated $300,000 per year, with over one-third coming from the state. Such relatively large fees could generally be supplemented with income from other employment since in most counties the job was not a full-time one.[36]

Probably because of the potential profitability of the office, many sought election to the jailership. In 1886 thirty-six vied for the Democratic nomination for jailer in Franklin County. Candidates in all counties campaigned strenuously, the incumbent jailer of Fayette County converting the vestibule of the courthouse into a bar serving "a sumptuous lunch, with ample toddy, and soberer drinks" for attendant "clients, lawyers, witnesses, judge, and jury" shortly before the election of 1870. In 1858 Democratic and American party nominees contested bitterly for the extremely lucrative jailership of Jefferson County, with the latter winning only after the Court of Appeals dismissed the former's charges of fraud on a technicality.[37]

Nineteenth-century Kentucky jailers apparently operated their jails fairly loosely with escapes not uncommon and other liberalities taken for granted. Although denying a charge that his jail was legally a "tippling house," Jacob Hackney of Laurel County admitted in 1876 that he allowed his prisoners a relatively free use of whiskey and that what spirits he did not provide himself could be readily purchased from others. There are also reported cases involving willful and negligent conduct on the part of jailers leading to escapes. And it was not uncommon for county courts to fine or grand juries to indict jailers for failure to keep their jails in a healthful and sanitary condition. Yet some jailers went beyond the call of duty, such as one in Kenton County who quit his trade as a blacksmith in order to afford special care to a sickly prisoner.[38]

Created by the framers of the third constitution, the assessor evaluated the property liable for state taxes, determined the names of all tithables, and performed various data-gathering functions, such as the number of births, marriages, and deaths within the county. For this he received fees averaging about $750 annually, a respectable income for a part-time government job. Like many county attorneys, assessors were frequently ambitious young men seeking a beginning to a bright political career. They, too, were often aligned with powerful families and assembled their own "squads" of political allies who would assist them in securing the assessor's office and aid them in future campaigns for more prestigious positions. Observers implied that many assessors undervalued taxable property because they had no business experience and because they wished to gain favor with voters in future elections. Such underassessment, of course, contributed to the chronic tax problems of late nineteenth-century Kentucky.[39]

Unlike the assessor, the office of coroner possessed a rich English and colonial heritage, but tradition did not reduce its deterioration. The coroner performed preliminary criminal enforcement duties, being bound to hold inquests upon the bodies of persons "slain, drown, or otherwise suddenly killed, or where any house be broken." If the coroner's jury found "any person . . . capable of murder, manslaughter, or of house-breaking, or of being accessory thereto," the coroner either arrested such person himself or had another law officer do it for him. The coroner also served as a substitute for the sheriff in case of a vacancy or conflict of interest.[40]

An office of little profit, the coronership in many counties became an object of near ridicule. When put up for the job by pranksters in Bourbon County in 1870, A. J. Lovely sarcastically withdrew from the race, claiming that he had recently been appointed Supervisor General "in the secret service of the I.O.K.O.S.P.," a position which commanded a salary of $100,000 per year and a free pass over all "rail and other roads, canals, rivers, lakes, bays, gulfs, seas and oceans within my jurisdiction." Fayette County Democrats offered to reward H. K. Milward, outgoing county coroner, with the nomination for sheriff because he had accepted the present office "solely to further the interests of . . . party . . . at considerable personal sacrifice." The office did not require a physician as occupant and those few who did seek it apparently did so often to have ready access to cadavers for experimentation. In some counties the position went unfilled.[41]

Similarly the office of constable degenerated into an almost empty sinecure. Essentially a process server and debt collector, constables were theoretically the administrative officers of justices of the peace and their judicial equivalents. There was usually one of them for every two justices. By statute they were required to serve civil summonses, peace and search warrants, levy attachments, summon garnishees, take up vagrants, summon witnesses, collect money under execution, collect fee-bills, summon and attend juries, kill mad dogs, kill and bury distempered animals, alter studs and bulls, apprehend alleged felons, and convey prisoners.[42]

Although there were seldom lively contests for the office, it did not go abegging as in the case of the coronership. Apparently several men sometimes agreed to divide the profits of the office, a practice much like that which frequently occurred during the period of the second constitution. On at least one occasion, a local businessman sought a constableship because he had personal debts outstanding of over $4,000 which he could collect cheaply and expeditiously in an official capacity.[43]

Because of their frequent contacts with persons in trouble with the law or creditors, constables sometimes encountered stiff opposition to the performance of their duties and on other occasions they themselves seemingly exceeded the proper bounds of conduct. In 1878 friends of the Reverend A. L. Jordan, a Harrison County Baptist minister, allegedly prevented R. A. King, constable for the Berryville Precinct, from levying on Jordan's coat and valise and aided Jordan in escaping to Ohio. In the same year, Mrs. Andrew Schlegel threw a bucket of water in the face of Frank Gosnell, a Jefferson County constable, and her husband threatened to kill him as he was trying to levy executions from a local magistrate's court. Gosnell was forced to enter the Schlegels' house by force and to throw Mrs. Schlegel on the ground and place his knee on her chest in order to accomplish his mission. In a subsequent legal action, a local judge fined Andrew Schlegel ten dollars for breach of peace and admonished Gosnell to execute his duties more gently. In other reported incidents, outraged citizens accused constables of every excess from illegal seizure and housebreaking to rape.⁴⁴

The remaining constitutionally created county officer, the surveyor, constituted the position of least significance within local government. Dutybound "to execute every order of survey made by any court of lands lying in his county, and make out and return a true plat and certificate thereof," the surveyor had increasingly less business and official income. Most, if not all, who sought the office, did so to bolster their own positions as private surveyors.⁴⁵

Although not mentioned in the constitution or a general statute, the office of county treasurer existed in a number of counties. Created by special legislative statute, the county treasurer normally collected monies from the sheriff and other "collecting officers" of the county and accounted for and banked same. In some cases treasurers had more limited duties, such as taking charge of all the county's internal improvement investments. Even though the practice was illegal in many, if not most, counties, local bankers bid on the right to be appointed treasurer by the county court, since the position allowed the bank to house county deposits. In Clark County, bankers bid as much as $1,500 for the right to serve as treasurer for one year.⁴⁶

Amazingly, despite seemingly impregnable legal barriers, women managed to crack the male monopoly of county offices, although most, if not all, served as deputies or in other subordinate positions. In 1885 Mrs. M. C. Lucas was elected to the jailership of Daviess County, only to have her election invalidated by the Court of Appeals on the grounds that the clear intention of the third constitution was to preclude women from serving in government. Some women did succeed in obtaining positions as deputies in various county offices, such as Fannie R. Bullock, who was appointed deputy county clerk of Fayette County in August 1882. In 1888 the legislature authorized what may have been an illegal practice by enacting a statute permitting county court clerks to appoint unmarried women as their deputies.⁴⁷

The democratic revolution of 1850, which saw framers of Kentucky's third constitution convert all its offices into elective positions, had little effect on the caliber of county government. Probably the constitution-makers succeeded most clearly in their invention of the county judge, who seemed to bring a semblance of judicial order out of what had often been complete chaos. County clerks generally performed with competence, but the tax collectors, process servers, legal document receivers, and criminal law enforcers enjoyed little public confidence. And they deserved little, being either personally incapable of performing efficiently or prevented by their statutory powers from functioning effectively.

3.
THE MAD SCRAMBLE FOR OFFICE

The reformers of 1849-1850 plunged county government into the thicket of elective politics. The Constitution of 1850 provided that all but two county officers were to be elected for four-year terms; the sheriff and constable were to be elected for two-year terms. By legislation elections for most county officers were held on the first Monday in August every four years beginning in 1854, the first being held in an odd year, 1851. For a time elections for justices of the peace and constables were held in May of odd-numbered years.[1]

Although Kentucky's first two-party system had reached full maturity by 1851, some observers hoped that party partisanship would not taint the politics of county government elections. Somewhat naively, the *Louisville Journal* argued that county offices were "not political, and the voters should not be influenced by partisan politics in filling them." On the eve of the county elections of 1851, the *Journal* found little indication of party activity, but warned that the Whigs would quickly enter the field should the Democrats attempt to organize. The Democrats remained aloof apparently, for in reporting the results of the race, the *Journal* mentioned no party labels, nor did any of the other Kentucky newspapers extant for that period.[2]

Such nonpartisanship unfortunately proved only temporary. While reported party conflict in 1854 involved only scattered elections, partisanship affected a majority of county contests in 1858. Of fifty-nine county races reported with sufficient particularity, thirty-seven matched Democrats versus American party aspirants, while in nineteen others parties contested over some but not all county offices. In only three counties did members of one party or the other capture races without meaningful party opposition. But in some counties, certain contests attracted two or more candidates from a single party, while others were uncontested. In Meade County, American party candidates for sheriff, county attorney, and surveyor ran unopposed; a Democrat opposed an American party candidate in each of the races for county judge and assessor; an American opposed another American aspirant for county clerk; two Americans opposed two Democrats for jailer; and two Americans opposed one Democrat for coroner. The situation was nearly as confused in Muhlenberg County. Similar conditions prevailed in at least eleven other counties. In some cases, more than one candidate from a single party doubtless entered county races at the urging, and even the connivance, of the rival party which desired to split the opposition. The *Louisville Democrat* reported that in Hart County "there was a vast amount of wire-working to defeat the nominees of the [Democratic] Party. Independent candidates from the Democratic ranks were induced to run, with a view to split and confuse the party, and thus contribute to the success of the Know-Nothing candidates."[3]

County elections seem to have become largely partisan by 1858 because each party was suspicious of the other's intentions and because party leaders and spokesmen believed that party activity at the local level would assist the party effort at the state and national levels. Experiences in Fayette and Franklin counties paralleled each other and highlighted the gradual politicization of county officeholding. Elections in both counties were nonpartisan in 1851, but on the eve of the 1854 election, each side accused the other of secret attempts to elect party slates put into the contests at the last minute. In both counties Democrats enjoyed more success in their eleventh-hour campaigns. But four years later, both parties organized openly well before the election and in each instance American party candidates won. The hope for nonpartisanship which had prevailed in 1851 and the public regret for the need for partisanship which had accompanied the secret machinations of 1854 had given way to blatant party organization in 1858. In the following year, the *Frankfort Commonwealth*, spokesman for the American party, doubtless sounded a commonly held notion when it urged party workers to continue to labor earnestly in local elections if for no other reason than because "the better fight we make for county officers, the greater service we do for the state ticket."[4]

Elections in 1862 apparently experienced a drastic decline in party activity. Few newspapers are extant for the period, and those report little party action in county elections, most of which involved "Union tickets." Kentucky's party system was in a definite state of transition at this time, and pro-Confederacy politicians doubtless were discouraged in their attempts to run for county office by the presence of Union troops and the decrees of their commanders specifying that only loyal citizens could run for office or vote. O. P. Hogan complained to Governor Beriah Magoffin that Union sympathizers in Grant County forced all candidates to join the "Union Party" and swear allegiance to same or drop out of the race. A correspondent to the *Louisville Journal* from Warren County reported that "there were no Southern Confederate candidates upon the track, as under the instructions of General Boyle.... they saw how utterly preposterous and contemptible it is for a man to ask office under a government towards which every thought and feeling ... is inimical."[5]

If the Civil War curtailed party activity at the county level, the coming of peace witnessed a sharp revival of local partisanship. Reports from fifty-four counties in 1866 indicate that in approximately 70 percent of them slates of candidates variously calling themselves conservative unionists, Republicans, or Independents vied with Democrats for county offices, while in two-thirds of the remaining counties several, but not all, of the offices were the objects of partisan contests. While antebellum

SCRAMBLE FOR OFFICE 45

Whig and American party candidates had closely contested Democratic candidates for county offices in most counties, in 1866 and ensuing elections Democrats won by far the largest share of the races. Such domination reflected a similar ascendency in contests for state and national offices. Only in southeastern Kentucky and in some eastern counties where Union sentiment had been strong in the war did Republicans enjoy general success.[6]

The ratification and hoped-for implementation of the Fifteenth Amendment prompted Republicans in many counties to wage all-out battles for control of county governments in the elections of 1870. Of seventy-eight reported elections, the vast majority involved Republican versus Democratic tickets. In several others, so-called Independents or Independent Democrats or both fought Regular Democrats for county offices. In Kenton County, a "Citizens' Party" vied with Independents and Democrats while in Meade County temporary factions favoring or opposing division of the county warred against one another. In Adair county, Democrats sometimes opposed each other for certain offices and in other races ran against candidates calling themselves Republicans or Conservatives. The Democracy in Cumberland County, according to a local correspondent to the *Courier-Journal*, "survived a most dangerous experiment" wherein twenty-two Democrats ran for eight offices with only four members of opposition parties in the field. Despite overwhelming support from thousands of blacks voting for the first time, Republicans made few inroads on Democratic county bastions.[7]

While party activity on the county level abated during the next six years, some spirited races did take place in certain areas. Contests in 1872 and 1874 for the sheriffalty of Fayette County, where large numbers of freedmen resided and voted for Republican candidates, were especially heated. Sensing that the Republican candidate, L. P. Tarlton, Jr., stood a good chance of winning the election, the Fayette County board of magistrates, all Democrats, threatened to appoint someone other than the sheriff as collector of the county levy should Tarlton win. Undaunted by these threats, Republicans worked feverishly for their candidate and secured a narrow victory. The Democratic threat proved idle (as well as illegal), and despite dire predictions of racial warfare and black supremacy, Tarlton proved to be a fair and competent sheriff. This did not deter Democrats from making a concerted effort to win back the office, which they did narrowly in 1874.[8]

Republicans in Mason County in 1874 adopted a strategy increasingly attractive to "out" parties. Labeling themselves "Independents," they campaigned vigorously against Democratic incumbents only to lose narrowly at the polls. Often in the minority, Republicans not infrequently wrapped themselves in the garb of "Independents," a tactic decried by Democrats who just as usually warned their party members to beware the phony lure of "Independence" and "no-partyism." Claiming that politics was "unimportant in county offices," Republicans in Lincoln County nonetheless nominated a candidate for county judge and elected him despite warnings by the dominant Democratic party that the opposition was trying to lull voters into nonpartisanship. In Gallatin County, Republicans entered a candidate for jailer at the last minute, hoping to take advantage of the fact that there were four Democrats in the field, but their ploy failed narrowly. In Bell County politics were at such a low ebb that neither party could "concentrate their men," and Democrats and Republicans held a joint convention to divide up nominations for county officers, pretending to be motivated by a desire to "select competent and qualified men from each of the parties alternately so as to avoid the trouble and excitement of heated political contests." In some counties in 1874, as in other elections, truly "Independent" slates competed with both Democrats and Republicans for county offices. According to the *Courier-Journal*, the Granger party ran a ticket in only one county, Pendleton, losing to the Democratic slate. Generally in that year's elections, fewer county races involved party politics, and appreciably more candidates faced no opposition in the general election.⁹

The National Greenback Labor party ran tickets in at least six counties in the 1878 elections but "cut no figure." Local partisan politics seemed to increase in that year, although many election clerks failed to send in returns for publication and county papers often neglected to designate the politics of candidates. In Montgomery County, Republicans ran a fusion ticket for jailer with Irish Democrats, they being angered by the defeat of their candidate in the Democratic primary; and in Hart the Grand Old Party took advantage of voter dissatisfaction with the results of the Democratic primary, but in most other counties outside of the southeastern section Democrats maintained their domination.¹⁰

Prohibitionists, usually composed mostly of Republicans, ran candidates for county offices for the first time in 1882, although their slates appeared in only a few counties. Candidates calling themselves Greenbackers ran in several counties in 1882, but none after that. In both the 1882 and 1886 elections the number of county contests with reported party activity vastly outnumbered races with little or no party conflict, and in most cases Democrats emerged victorious with Republicans securing most of their wins in their traditional strongholds.¹¹

County elections on the eve of constitutional reform in 1890 are especially significant because the degree of party participation was reported for over two-thirds of them, the most complete sampling of any election. These sources indicate that party activity continued to dominate most elections, existing to a marked extent in over three-fourths of the races reported. In most contests, Republican slates opposed the majority Democratic party candidates, but in some Prohibitionists and the ever-present Independents formed either the major source of opposition or one of two major sources. And for the first time, candidates from the newly organized Farmers' Alliance party appeared in a few elections. The election in Bracken County proved particularly heated with Republicans, buoyed by individual successes in recent elections, fielding nearly a full slate against the dominant Democrats only to "encounter a Waterloo." But in normally Democratic Hopkins County, Republicans were able to take advantage of dissension within the majority ranks over the results of a controversial primary and the question of prohibition, to secure the county attorneyship and closely contest other offices.[12]

Lack of party conflict in county elections did not necessarily mean lack of candidates for office. If dominant parties held primaries or nominating conventions, these affairs were usually crowded with would-be nominees. Nor would disappointed candidates always abide by the results of the party's nominating process. Such disappointed suitors frequently continued their pursuit of office, running as independents against regular party nominees. Sometimes majority parties facing no appreciable opposition from "out" parties had no formal nominations, and general elections featured four or five or more candidates for each office. By 1878 critics perceived an obsession motivating hordes of persons to seek county office who "would not otherwise descend into the cesspool of politics." In the opinion of the *Boone County Recorder* many felt driven to seek office "in the hope of being aided in providing for their families by the salaries paid these offices." Ironically, the paper noted, the least lucrative offices seemed to attract the greatest number of candidates. A correspondent from Green County reported that a majority of the candidates for county office in 1878 focused attention on their financial needs rather than their qualifications for office. Even more cynical about the process, the *Kentucky Gazette* argued that "the struggle for office is one of the most disgusting and disgraceful phases that politics has ever assumed and is fast driving the most respectable . . . citizens into private life, leaving only the hardened, selfish, and unqualified to continue the frantic contest." The mad scramble for office produced overly lengthy campaigns which sometimes began in mid-winter even though elections were not held until

August. The *Gazette* sarcastically noted in February 1878 that "candidates are thick as corn-cobs around a county school house . . . they all want to serve the dear people, their county, and themselves in particular. . . . for each office there are about ten aspirants and everyone sanguine that he will be the lucky man." By July 1878 the *Gazette* was calling for shorter campaigns, arguing that the existing system harassed candidates and voters alike.[13]

If competition for most county offices remained lively, if not always the subject of interparty conflict, throughout the period of the third constitution, interest in the offices of justice of the peace and constable lagged in many places. Political parties seldom made formal nominations for these positions, although in a number of races individual candidates ran as partisans. Newspaper editors periodically chided parties and voters for paying scant attention to the office of justice of the peace and noted the significance of the court of claims, but this made little impact on the prevailing condition of apathy.

The presence of heated two-party confrontations in many of the county elections meant that often the paramount issue of campaigns amounted to nothing more than which party could command the most loyalty from its members. In others, economic issues complicated the process. These ranged from controversies over fiscal management and accountability to disputes over allegedly inflated salaries or the necessity for special taxes for such improvements as railroad construction. Following the war, prohibition became more and more of an issue in certain county elections. Occasionally ethnic considerations prevailed in individual races, such as in Mason County in 1874 and 1878 where Democrats seriously divided over the demands by some for a jailer of Irish extraction and in Montgomery County in 1878, where Republicans joined with dissident Democrats to promote the candidacy of an Irishman defeated in a bitter primary fight for the Democratic nomination for jailer.[14]

Intense competition for county office contributed to the

generally corrupt and sometimes oppressive nature of Kentucky politics in the second half of the nineteenth century. Before 1850 the most flagrant example of county political fraud concerned the sale of offices, most normally that of the sheriffalty, county clerkship, and constableships for prices ranging from $6,000 for the clerkship of a populous county to a few hundred dollars for a minor constableship. Following 1850, when most county offices were elective and not appointive as before, the simple sale of office became virtually impossible. Only in those few cases where offices continued to be appointive, as county treasurerships and deputy sheriffalties, did the practice continue. Although technically in violation of the state law against the sale or farming of public office, it was common practice for boards of magistrates to sell the office of county treasurer to the highest bidder (usually a banker). Likewise the profits of the sheriffalty were frequently divided up among the high sheriff and his deputies. Prosecutions of these offenses occurred infrequently.[15]

The absence of outright sale of offices did not mean that considerable sums of money were not used to influence the outcome of elections to the most lucrative of county offices. Even after the reforms of 1849-1850, voting continued to be done by voice rather than secret ballot. Each voter would proclaim his preferences before the precinct sheriff and the assembled officials, plus all who wished to hear his declaration. The lack of secrecy meant that candidates, politicians, and parties could keep running tabulations of how each race was evolving, and could determine how each man had cast his vote. Such openness helped contribute to the tendency of aspiring politicians to purchase the assistance of professional wire-pullers who in turn rounded up votes, oftentimes buying them.

More than a few observers of Kentucky's elections commented that vote-buying was commonplace and some even called for its termination. Following the county elections of 1882, the *Courier-Journal* observed almost casually that "there was nothing noticeable about the manner of the contest. The usual number of purchasable bummers swarmed about the candidates and their friends and exacted their pound of flesh.... the features of the day were rather ordinary.... the floater was paid his price.... thousands of respectable citizens were crowded away from the polls by purchasable hoodlums." A new resident of turbulent Rowan County testifed that the price of a vote in his county ranged from $2.50 to $50, "with the price increasing as close of election approached." The smart seller held back until the polls were about to close. Having only recently moved to Kentucky, the Rowan countian also commented that he had never seen a man sell his vote until he had moved to Kentucky. Levi Grow, justice of the peace for the district of South Elkhorn in Fayette County "made a big hit" at a political rally in July 1890, "when he expressed the belief that every officeholder in the county, except himself and a few other magistrates, had secured their offices by use of money, either at a primary or general election." In the same year, the Republican *Lexington Leader* accused a Montgomery County candidate for county office of importing thugs from Fayette to buy votes in order to win a closely contested election. Despite the illegality of such practices, violators were seldom prosecuted, and the only recorded cases involving vote-buying heard by the Court of Appeals were civil actions attempting to invalidate elections because of the vote-buying or loans made to purchase votes.[16]

Candidates for county office freely applied intoxicating beverages to wavering voters and often almost literally floated to victory. Election days frequently were the scenes of drunken orgies. The Republicans of Grayson County mustered a record vote when in 1886 they rented a saloon and set up a free bar. A correspondent from Spring Lick (also in Grayson County) reported that the whole town was drunk during the elections of 1882. The *Barbourville Mountain Echo* reported that some of the county candidates of Knox County on the court day preceding the 1874 elections "were trying, most laboriously, to float into office by way of the groceries, and at the floodtide of drunkenness." Seeking to counteract the traditionally free use of whiskey at their county elections, Prohibitionists in Clark County dispensed free ice cream at the polls.[17]

Election-day drunkenness and competitiveness meant fights as well as votes. Newspaper accounts of county elections contain widespread reports of fistfights, knifings, and shootings. In one precinct alone of Green County, a deputy sheriff shot it out with an aggrieved black voter, "social knock-downs were in progress all day," miscellaneous shootings and stabbings were reported and two factions peered at one another throughout the day with shotguns firmly in place. At a Franklin County precinct in 1890, excitement ran so high "it was feared there would be a general riot, but the night closed with about twenty knockdowns and an affray between six or seven whites and blacks packed in a crowd of two hundred people in which knives, clubs, pistols, and stones were freely used." A correspondent to the *Courier-Journal* reported "only four fights" in Boyle County's election of 1878 and a writer from Ohio twelve years later noted with some evident surprise that no one had been killed in his county's election.[18]

Fisticuffs amounted to voter intimidation in some county elections. Democrats accused Franklin County Americans of attempting to keep Irish voters from the polls in the hotly contested elections of 1854 and 1858, while in 1890 Republicans accused Democrats of Clark County of importing toughs from Lexington to browbeat voters into submission. A special election in Franklin County in 1863 featured rival gangs attempting to out-intimidate each other and the voters.[19]

Sometimes county officials themselves played major roles in voter frauds and intimidation. Taking advantage of a recently enacted election law requiring the appointment of precinct sheriffs and clerks from different political parties, the Democratic Franklin county judge on the eve of the 1858 county elections appointed a member of the American party clerk of the Frankfort precinct so that the county sheriff, also a member of the American party, could not serve as election sheriff of his own precinct. Outraged, the *Frankfort Commonwealth,* newspaper of the American party, accused the county judge of attempting to remove the sheriff from the election process so that Democrats could successfully import voters from neighboring counties, a ploy that the American sheriff had allegedly prevented in 1855 and 1856. Faced with arguments that his actions violated the spirit of the new law, the county judge reneged. Ironically, following the August election, Democrats complained that Americans intimidaged voters at the polls.[20]

Generally avid interest in securing county office meant commensurate interest in the nominating process. While the reformers of 1849-1850 provided for popularly elected county officers, they did not specify the method of nomination. During the first two decades of the third constitution, county committees and conventions determined party nominations for county offices. Usually composed of prominent men in the community, the county committee was not a democratic institution but rather appointed by the state party committee. While not much information exists regarding its functions, in many counties it often determined the mode of nominations to county office. Until the period following the Civil War, county committees normally decreed that county conventions should nominate candidates for county office. Often, committees further ruled that precinct conventions should elect delegates to the county conventions. County committees sometimes took informal control of general elections, sending agents throughout the county to poll voters and rally the faithful in order to "know the exact status of the party as to the number of its votes." Active county committees usually possessed an energetic chairman, such as James F. Robinson, who helped revitalize the Democratic party in Fayette County after 1865.[21]

Following the Civil War, politicians and voters began to complain about "rings," "cliques," and "tricksters," all of whom were allegedly dominating the rather closed system of party nominations. Some of this criticism singled out county committees for reform. In 1871 dissident Democrats called for popular election of the Harrison County committee on the grounds that the state committee consisted of "self-constituted political jugglers" who named only residents of Cynthiana to the local committee. But most critics made less specific charges, referring vaguely to "court house cliques" which allegedly were more interested in perpetuating their own power than serving the interests of the people.[22]

Despite considerable hullaballoo to the contrary, some observers saw accusations about "tricksters" as nothing more than the complaints of would-be county officers trying to oust those in power. Calling such clamor a great "bug-a-boo," the *Hickman Courier* wrote in 1878 that there was much "unnecessary excitement about 'rings.' They are often alleged to exist when they do not exist; they often exist when there is no harm in their existence." According to the *Courier*, rings were often "the natural product of local politics—a war of the outs against the ins and the ins against the outs. But, of course, the candidates expect the people to shout themselves hoarse about these things." As if to bear out the *Courier*'s analysis, newspaper editors and politicians engaged in lengthy debates in such counties as Harrison and Mason following the Civil War over whether courthouse rings did exist, and if so, how much influence they possessed.[23]

Real or imaginary, rings aroused sufficient opposition in many counties to produce successful movements for party nominations by popular primary. Proponents of the primary argued that professional politicians, adept at rhetoric and parliamentary procedure, dominated party conventions and that the rank and file seldom attended. But reformers did not secure popular primaries without opposition and controversy continued after their adoption. Battles in Franklin, Fulton, Bourbon, Fayette, Mason, Pendleton, and Harrison counties following the Civil War illustrate the intensity and realities of the struggle.

Most of the available evidence concerning the evolution of the popular primary in Kentucky involves the Democratic party. Although Republicans apparently did adopt the primary in some counties, especially where they were the dominant party, in many counties they continued to use the convention method. On the other hand, Democrats, especially in those counties where they were the dominant party, which was often the case, exhibited a greater willingness to experiment with popular primaries.

In the late spring of 1866, Clark County Democrats apparently became the first party organization to adopt the popular primary as their method of nominating county officers. Although little is known about the origins of the Clark County primary, a neighboring newspaper reported that the county committee adopted the new method in order to "harmonize the discordant elements in the county." Evidently successful, the Clark County reform served as an impetus for a similar experiment in Bourbon County two years later when the county committee there announced that a primary election would determine county officer nominees. But the Bourbon County Democratic Committee presumably had second thoughts about the scheme, for in the following spring it opted for the more familiar convention system as the method of selecting a legislative candidate. This decision sparked widespread demands for the permanent adoption of the popular primary on the grounds that the county committee represented a "Paris clique of a half dozen men to control and suppress the voice of the Democracy." Threatened by a movement to elect delegates to the convention who would refuse to vote for any nominee, the committee reneged and ordered a primary to be held. By 1874 primaries constituted the normal way to nominate Democratic candidates for Bourbon County office.[24]

After sporadic agitation for and against the reform, Fayette County Democrats tried the experiment for the first time in early 1870, initially nominating city officer candidates, then county. But the county committee's commitment was temporary, and it revived the convention system for most of the party county nominations for the remainder of the decade. A very bitter dispute arising from the county nominating convention of June 1878 renewed demands for a return to the popular primary. A maverick Democrat (A. M. Harrison) upset incumbent A. G. Hunt for the party's nomination for county clerk when two delegates from the Sandersville precinct violated the instructions of their precinct convention and voted against Hunt. This prompted a leading Democratic newspaper of the county to describe nominating conventions as collections of "little men" whose only successes in life occurred in the "cesspool of the primary convention" at the expense of sober, modest gentlemen. Amid a storm of protest, two delegates shortly afterwards acknowledged their heresy, causing the county committee to call a special convention, which nominated Hunt over the protestations of Harrison supporters. Seizing the moment, Republicans ran an independent against Hunt in the general election and nearly won the election. Thereafter, the county committee normally adopted the popular primary as its method of determining party candidates for county office. So intense was dissatisfaction with the traditional method of nomination in Franklin County, that in 1869 the Democratic nominating convention itself called attention to its own deficiencies and suggested, at a minimum, that the county committee initiate reforms in delegate selection. Most nominations for county officers thereafter resulted from popular primaries. Fulton County Democrats experienced a similar revulsion to conventions in 1876 and soon after joined the tide of change.[25]

Similarly Mason County Democrats warred over the method of nominating county officers as a part of a general power struggle which featured rival Maysville newspapers, the *Republican* representing the insurgents and the *Bulletin* speaking for the establishment. Blasted for nearly ten years by the *Republican* for its oligarchical ways, the county committee finally adopted a popular primary in 1878. Although reluctantly acquiescing in the move, the *Bulletin* found the experience altogether unfortunate and launched a largely unsuccessful campaign to return the party to conventions.[26]

By 1880 numerous other county party organizations had commenced nominating by popular primary, but the reform movement, which was initially an intraparty affair, encountered such hostility in some quarters that moderate legislative intervention was needed. From the outset, primaries possessed detractors. Labeling the concept a "Yankee institution," the *Maysville Bulletin* argued that "cliques, rings and tricksters" would prevail no matter what system of nomination was adopted. Popular primaries only promoted divisiveness within the party, encouraged public drunkenness, allowed the opposition party to influence party nominations by encouraging their members to vote illegally, and permitted candidates with only a minority of the votes to run in the general election. Other voices echoed these charges and noted that weak candidates could easily win nominations.[27]

Pendleton County's Democratic primary of 1878 seemed to confirm the worst predictions of the reform's critics. Describing the occasion as not a primary but a "general election . . . in which voters of all political shades and men of all colors and citizens of various counties voted, and the candidates who could use the most money and whiskey, import[ed] the most votes for hire," the *Falmouth Independent* predicted that many Democrats would vote against the party's nominees. By June the *Independent*'s prediction began to bear fruit as slates of "Independent Democrats" appeared for all county offices, even some for the usually ignored justice of the peace. Others, citing proof that nearly half of the voters in the primary had been Republicans, minors, blacks, aliens, and nonresidents, demanded unsuccessfully that the county committee call a new convention to screen primary candidates as a prelude to a new primary election. Although extant records do not reveal the winners of the general election, it is clear that the primary of 1878 severely disrupted the harmony of Pendleton's Democracy.[28]

The initially popular primary of the Mason County Democracy produced similar fireworks. Only a grudging participant in the election, the editor of the *Maysville Bulletin* branded the affair as an "instrumentality for the demoralization of the party.... and affording temptations for fraud, corruption and vice.... there never was at any election within our memory, so many drunken men at the polls, as there were in the city on Monday." Alleging that several primary winners had received only a small fraction of the total votes and that the reform had been adopted in the first place in response to outcries against a "mythical ring," the journalist vowed to oppose future primaries which, if they continued, would "end in the annihilation of the party that adopts it."[29]

While opponents of popular primaries in many counties were unable to defeat the reform, detractors in Harrison County secured at least a temporary delay in the change. Early in 1868 the *Cynthiana News* commenced a two-year campaign to persuade the Democratic county committee to adopt the popular primary system of nominations. Citing support from candidates as well as masses of voters, the *News* argued that primaries would permit the "reticent farmer" to gain equality with the "orators and manipulators" who had dominated the party's conventions. Early in 1870 the committee ordered a primary to nominate candidates for county office and again in 1872 ordered one to nominate for the sheriffalty. Ironically, at the next primary in 1873 opponents of the plan succeeded in placing the question of its retention on the ballot and defeated it, 685 to 892. But the setback proved only temporary, and by 1880 the county committee restored the popular primary on a generally permanent basis.[30]

Despite their lack of success, critics of the popular primary correctly assessed its basic weaknesses in its early stages. In order to correct these deficiencies, some county party committees revised procedures on their own; others reformed with the assistance of local legislation. The Jefferson County Democratic Committee devised a registration system which attempted to insure that only loyal Democrats participated in the county's popular primary. Each new voter had to register at party headquarters, signing an affidavit that he, if eligible, had voted for the previous Democratic presidential candidate and intended to support Democratic nominees of the next primary election. Between 1880 and 1890, sixteen counties secured special legislation enabling political parties at their discretion to establish similar laws of registration and providing criminal sanctions against those who violated party rules. Not until June 1892 did the legislature enact a mandatory law regulating party primaries in all counties.[31]

The introduction of democratic voting and nominating procedures posed new problems and challenges to Kentucky's county politicians. At first they scrambled for office without the aid of political parties, but the opportunities for organized effort soon proved too alluring; by the end of the first decade of the new constitution, Democrats and Americans were in the thick of it. Following the Civil War, local politicos groped with the problem of how best to nominate candidates for county office and non-Democratic party candidates struggled against a Democracy that dominated the governments of most Kentucky counties.

4.
CONSTITUTIONAL CONVULSION AND CONFRONTATION

No event highlighted the semi-autonomous nature of Kentucky's counties more than the Civil War. Although the Commonwealth itself remained in the Union, individual counties and their officers and governments conducted themselves in ways approaching secession. The war also disrupted the functioning of county governments and their officials, necessitating emergency legislation and much improvisation.

Although there is no evidence that the abortive pro-rebel Provisional Government of Kentucky created county governments to aid in its secessionist activities, there is some indication that individual county officers aided the Confederate cause. Because it had been represented to the General Assembly "that in some of the counties ... the judges of county courts and sheriffs [had] ... adhered to, sympathized with, and given aid and countenance to" the Provisional Government and refused to carry out their duties to the regularly constituted government in Frankfort, the legislature in March 1862 felt compelled to allow by statute the governor to replace such dissidents by special election after only two "loyal resident freeholders" swore by affidavit to their disloyal conduct. In the same month, the legislature authorized the Commonwealth to proceed against county officers illegally collecting state taxes for use by the Provisional Government.[1]

Early in the course of the war, rebel sympathizers forced certain county officers to swear allegiance to the Provisional Government. On the other hand, G. A. Flournoy, county judge of McCracken County, refused to take an oath to the federal government, which included a pledge to "surrender the right of trial by jury" if prosecuted for alleged disloyalty. Despite this refusal, Flournoy continued in office throughout the war. In Wolfe County, unspecified persons prevented the county judge from holding court between September 1861 and April 1862 because he was a suspected southern sympathizer. A loyal justice of the peace finally purported to hold court in April 1862 and appointed a new sheriff, constable, "and other officers to fill the vacancies of officers which have resigned or are considered as disloyal." But some entertained doubts as to the legality of the justice's action, taxes remained uncollected, and county government had almost ceased to function, prompting several to seek guidance from the governor.[2]

Military activities disrupted normal county governmental activity and caused the legislature to enact laws to remedy emergency situations. The General Assembly extended deadlines when rebel forces prevented the officers of various counties from taking prescribed oaths "at the times fixed by law," and obstructed numbers of sheriffs from executing bond in a timely fashion. Especially harassed were sheriffs who benefited from statutes extending the period in which to collect county and state taxes and making it a "sufficient return" to swear that the presence of guerrilla bands made it impossible to execute process or collect money.[3]

The war produced more vacancies in county offices than at any other time in Kentucky's history. In McCracken County, a hotbed of rebel activity in western Kentucky, the newly elected county attorney, county court clerk, and coroner failed to qualify for office after the August 1862 elections. By 1865 civil affairs were so disrupted in eastern Kentucky's Letcher County that there were no county officers and the governor had to appoint a county judge until one could be elected. The statute books and county court order books are filled with acts authorizing special appointments and elections and orders implementing them.[4]

County courts, whether county judges sitting as probate or quarterly court tribunals or courts of claims, and justices of the peace sometimes found it difficult to hold sessions at regularly scheduled times. Frequently the General Assembly suspended courts or enabled county courts to have jurisdiction over neighboring counties where courts could not sit. The county and quarterly courts of Harlan County were given jurisdiction over probate and civil matters in adjacent Letcher and Perry counties, "no ... courts having been held ... for more than twelve months prior hereto, causing thereby much loss and inconvenience to many persons." In other counties, such as McCracken, county courts and other tribunals simply had to find different places to hold sessions because federal troops had occupied courthouses for hospital and other purposes.[5]

Initially state officials encouraged counties to cooperate with federal efforts to prosecute the war against the South, but as policies and popular moods in the state changed and the Union was increasingly perceived by Kentuckians as the aggressor and the South the victim, attitudes on the issue of county cooperation also changed. In August 1861 Governor Beriah Magoffin, despite his pro-southern sympathies, directed all county judges to make a "diligent" search for all arms, equipment, and munitions belonging to the state "not ... in the hands of lawfully organized military companies" and return them to the State Arsenal. Several months later, the General Assembly directed county judges, justices of the peace, and other judicial officers to issue arrest warrants for the apprehension of alleged deserters from the federal army and instructed sheriffs, coroners, justices of the peace, and policemen to arrest and turn them over to military authorities. But by 1864 state policy had changed. Governor Thomas Bramlette secured a presidential recision of General Hugh Ewing's order that the county courts of every county levy a tax sufficient to raise and equip fifty federal troops within each county. Early in the next year, at the urgings of the counties themselves, the legislature permitted several county courts to levy a tax to pay for bounties or substitutes in order that male residents might avoid the draft laws.[6]

War also interfered with county elections. In rebellious counties where sheriffs and other county officials refused to hold elections, private citizens were empowered by the legislature to do so and to submit the poll books to the governor. The presence of federal troops in some counties resulted in challenges to election results. In McCracken County, J. B. Hinton sued J. K. Leeman, the apparent winner of a special election for county clerk, on the grounds that federal troops had initimidated voters, but Leeman remained in office after the Court of Appeals ruled that Hinton had pursued the wrong form of action. In other counties, aggrieved candidates were known to accuse officials of conspiring with federal troops to violate the rights of certain citizens. In one notorious incident of this nature, the General Assembly determined in 1865 that the Madison county judge had illegally compiled a list of allegedly disloyal county residents and successfully urged federal troops to prevent them from voting.[7]

Stormy days for Kentucky counties did not end with the termination of the Civil War. The Commonwealth and its counties continued their tentative relationship with the federal government and most especially regarded the presence of the Freedmen's Bureau as a hostile imposition to be resisted at all costs. Befitting the children of a parent who refused to ratify the Thirteenth, Fourteenth, and Fifteenth amendments, Kentucky's counties and their officials resisted federal efforts to amalgamate freedmen into postwar society and instead created their own special brand of quasi-servitude.

Congress's decision to extend the jurisdiction of the Freedmen's Bureau to Kentucky and other border states, which remained theoretically loyal to the federal government, stemmed from the presence there of thousands of newly emancipated blacks. Two of the bureau's most important functions were to aid black orphans and apprentices and assist black paupers. Although the bureau maintained over twenty-five field offices in the Commonwealth for approximately three years and espoused lofty goals of economic and cultural uplifting, the success of its orphan, apprentice, and pauper programs depended largely on cooperation from county governments. In all but a few counties cooperation was not forthcoming or only given grudgingly.

Congress had charged the Freedmen's Bureau with the task of insuring that black orphans and indigent children were fairly and adequately apprenticed. Declaring on October 4, 1865, that "officers of this bureau are regarded as guardians of orphans, minors or freedmen within their respective districts," Major General O. O. Howard, commissioner of the bureau, instructed his personnel to recognize state apprenticeship laws "provided they make no distinction of color." Elaborating upon these guidelines, Brigadier General Clinton B. Fisk, head of the bureau's district for Kentucky, Tennessee, and northern Alabama, specified on October 10 of the same year that in all apprenticeship cases bureau agents should secure acknowledgment of indentures from county courts. Masters had to promise to feed, clothe, and train each apprentice and had to be persons of good character and reputation, who, if they had been slave owners, had not maltreated their slaves. Ordinarily males would be apprenticed until twenty-one and females until eighteen, and every minor fourteen and over would have the right of choosing his or her own master. Indigent parents had to give their consent to the apprenticing of their children.[8]

While bureau officials (at least for the record) deemed their assignment one of cooperation with state officials in the provision and care of black minors, Kentucky's political and judicial leaders, both on the state and county level, regarded the presence of federal authorities on their soil as a massive encroachment on traditionally local business and did their utmost to resist this interference. The General Assembly in February

1866 made it a duty of county courts in apprenticeship cases involving freedmen to give preference to their former owners if the owners should request it, provided they were "suitable" persons. Eagerly seizing upon this statute, former owners and county courts commenced apprenticing masses of black children regardless of the status of their parentage or economic situation, perpetuating, in the opinion of bureau officials, "a species of slavery by authority of apprenticeship."[9]

Initially, bureau agents in Kentucky sought to counteract the proliferation of postwar quasi-slavery by dealing directly with county courts and masters, securing as many legitimate indentures of apprenticeship as possible and simultaneously undoing the collusive and oppressive contracts sanctioned by the courts under the statute of 1866. Both tasks proved difficult. In the years 1866 and 1867, agents apprenticed on the average only about twenty children per month and in 1868, the final year of apprenticing, obtained only a handful of indentures, while some county courts acting under the state law and without bureau participation, approved over a hundred contracts in a single year. The field officer for Russell, Wayne, and Adair counties lamented that while there were "a good many orphans and abandoned children" in his area, he found "it impossible to apprentice them to good masters."[10]

Upon learning of a coercive apprenticeship, bureau officials moved to secure voluntary dissolution of the contract and the return of the child to his parents, if living, or apprenticeship to a more suitable master. Not surprisingly the majority of such cases involved children of living parents, since orphans presumably found it difficult to notify the bureau of their grievances. In Boone County, one Willis Street was accused of possessing the two daughters of John Finney without his permission and was requested to produce his authority for doing so. Similar requests went to Mrs. Green Mudd of Marion County in relation to the children of "Alice" and to Mrs. Caroline Murphy (residence not indicated) with respect to Susannah Hobbs, daughter of Else Hobbs. The bureau accused Jack Dickinson not only of possessing thirteen-year-old Lucien Scott (Dickinson) from March 1865 to April 1866, but of maltreating him and of refusing to compensate his mother for his services. Similarly, agents charged N. R. Black of Crittenden County of apprenticing two children of Mingo Clements without his permission.[11]

In other cases, officers of Kentucky's bureau instructed field superintendents to deal directly with county judges who had apprenticed blacks in violation of bureau regulations. For example, on the first day of September 1866, Levi Burnett instructed John L. Peyton, superintendent of the Madisonville office, to "call upon" the judge of Hopkins County and request that he cancel an indenture apprenticing a black child to Mrs. Bathsheba W. Cox without consent of her relatives, taking with him "the nearest relative of the girl." Other county court judges, such as those for Cumberland, Clinton, and Monroe counties, did in fact apprentice blacks to "good families" without much urging by bureau agents. But most judges followed the lead of Bourbon county judge Richard Hawes, who in early 1867 ruled in the case of the children of former slave Harriet Hurley that the Freedmen's Bureau Act did not apply to Kentucky and that all contracts of apprenticeship made by bureau agents in the state were "null and void." Even though Hawes's ruling represented a flagrant misreading of the statutory law and was undoubtedly overruled if appealed (no evidence exists as to the outcome of such a proceeding), it nonetheless signified the beliefs and practices of most of his colleagues in other counties.[12]

County court records generally confirm appraisals of the bureau. Entries for the years 1866 through 1868 for ten counties with slightly over 25 percent of the state's freedmen indicate that the county courts therein apprenticed 553 black children. Most children were apprenticed without parental consent, although many were orphans. Five counties noted whether masters had been previous owners, and of 320 apprenticeships, 200 involved the former owners of those children. The ten county courts canceled seventeen indentures and only one at the behest of the bureau, although two others were subjects of show-cause orders apparently never executed. Of the ten sample counties, Christian County possessed the second most freedmen (9,812) and apprenticed more blacks (205), apprenticed more to former owners (159), and canceled more indentures (9) than any of the other nine counties. On the other hand, while Boyle County in central Kentucky possessed substantial numbers of freedmen (3,679), the order books indicate that the county court apprenticed only a few children.[13]

By early 1867 bureau officials in Kentucky realized that their policy of dealing directly with former slave owners and county courts in an attempt to undo harsh indentures of apprenticeship had proved a dismal failure. The monthly report for February 1867 indicated that county courts, especially in the western and northwestern subdistricts, were indiscriminately binding out blacks to their former owners regardless "of age or condition" and that many of these masters were in turn hiring out their new charges to third parties in violation of the indentures. Shortly thereafter, bureau officials hired prominent Louisville attorney and former United States Attorney General James Speed to contest the validity of the Kentucky statute of 1866. By October 1867 Speed had advised bureau officials that county courts could not validly bind out black children under the statute of 1866 if the indentures discriminated against them because of color and advised bureau chiefs to encourage aggrieved freedmen to seek writs of habeas corpus from federal court. In early 1868 bureau officials reported that they were following Speed's prescription and that the federal court was invalidating discriminatory indentures for most freedmen who applied to it for relief. Regrettably for apprenticed freedmen, the bureau exaggerated the impact of the federal court on their plight. While relevant records for the federal court for the eastern district of Kentucky are not extant, records for the court for the western district sitting primarily in Louisville reveal that that tribunal afforded only minimal relief to black apprentices.

Between September 1866 and November 1869 the court heard only eleven petitions seeking dissolution of apprenticeships, with all of them being decided between May 1867 and February 1868. Although the court ruled in favor of the apprentice in every case, eleven dissolutions out of several thousand apprenticeships hardly represents a major victory for the bureau and freedmen against the connivances of the county courts and former slave owners.[14]

Bureau officials in Kentucky also tried to insure that impoverished freedmen received adequate care by cooperating with county officials, the traditional dispensers of poor relief. But, as in the case with apprentices, the bureau claimed to receive little cooperation from the counties, despite the passage by the legislature of a statute providing special funds for black poor relief. Apparently some recommended challenging alleged county intransigence in federal court, but no one did so, and throughout its brief sojourn in Kentucky, the bureau did little more than lament these apparent transgressions.

Initially it appeared that the bureau and counties would cooperate in providing for the black poor. Bureau leaders instructed agents to refer all cases of pauperism to county courts and to encourage the tribunals to permit former masters to aid their "aged and infirm" former slaves. In February 1866 the General Assembly passed a statute requiring county courts to collect a two-dollar capitation tax on all black males over the age of eighteen, requiring them to use the funds for poor relief and education. But by the late spring of 1866 bureau officials were complaining that while counties were collecting the tax, few of them were using the funds for their intended purposes. Nor would many of the county judges furnish a list of destitute freedmen and refugees in their counties as requested by the bureau.[15]

In the opinion of bureau officials, conditions deteriorated in the following year. The chief agent at Owensboro in Ohio County complained that courts of claims in his district applied tax funds exclusively for the benefit of former slave owners who wished to retain former household slaves. In response to an inquiry from Colonel Benjamin P. Runkle, who believed that the counties should be forced to apply funds for their intended purpose or stop collecting the tax, James Speed recommended that the bureau first seek legislative repeal of the statute and, if that failed, its judicial invalidation. The legislature did not repeal the statute until 1871, after the bureau ceased to function as an agency for poor blacks in the state. While the bureau continued to accuse counties of misapplying funds, it apparently never filed suit to stop the pernicious practice.[16]

Entries in the order books of ten sample counties possessing slightly over one-fourth of the state's freedmen suggest that Freedmen's Bureau officials may have exaggerated the extent of county inequities in the creation and implementation of black pauper policy. In six counties, black paupers received aid from early 1866 through the period of the Freedmen's Bureau. In the remaining four, impoverished freedmen initially received only sporadic aid, but by 1868 benefited from more charitable distributions of the dole. Of course, the official records do not reveal whether county courts favored former masters as the bureau alleged. Naturally, too, even the most generous counties normally made relief payments to freedmen only from the special fund raised by the black head tax; and when those funds proved inadequate, payments had to be scaled down.[17]

Bureau intentions regarding black vagrants likewise initially seemed to coincide with state and county policy. Brigadier General Fisk's instructions of late 1865 specified that agents turn over to county authorities all freedmen who "neglected to apply themselves to an honest calling, or sauntered about neglecting their business, or . . . maintained themselves by gaming or other dishonest means, or quartered themselves upon industrious and well-behaved persons." Fisk's language closely resembled that of Kentucky's vagrancy statute which required county officials to arrest and circuit courts to "sell into servitude" (or apprentice if the defendant was a minor) all "able-bodied persons . . . found loitering or rambling about, not having the means to maintain himself, by some visible property" or who does not work or make an honest effort to find work. But the implementation of the state statute by county officers and circuit court judges and juries soon dispelled any hope for cooperation with the bureau. No longer concerned so much with the "credit and well-being of the industrious" and the "peace and good order of the community," bureau agents by 1868 contemplated action against county officials who were allegedly "taking up" many freedmen and selling them as alleged vagrants into a type of neoslavery. As in its response to county policy regarding black paupers, bureau officers confined their reaction to the vagrancy problem by privately anguishing rather than bringing suit in the federal district court, or instigating some other effective action.

On January 1, 1869, the Freedmen's Bureau terminated most of its business in Kentucky. During its brief sojourn within the Commonwealth, its activity amounted to an incomplete holding action due mainly to the stubborn refusal of the counties to accept the presence of federal involvement in local affairs. While not always able to govern their own special units effectively, county officials practiced resistance with precision and thereby largely frustrated the only major intervention into Kentucky's affairs by the federal government during peacetime in the nineteenth century. Simultaneously the counties insured the continuation of Kentucky's enduring constitutional parochialism, as well as the preservation of her social order.

5.
LAW AND ORDER

Never a state committed to domestic tranquillity, Kentucky's lawlessness reached prodigious proportions during and after the Civil War. Summing up the course of criminality during the previous twenty years, the *New York Times* reported in 1883 that "probably there is no state in which lawlessness and bloodshed prevail to such an outrageous extent as in Kentucky, and there certainly is no state in which the laws against crime are so feebly executed." Popular outcries against crime and the lack of law enforcement constituted a major impetus for the constitutional convention of 1890-1891. Would-be reformers debated the issue "at almost every voting place" in the state, and delegates at the convention strove earnestly to cope with a problem that some equated with anarchy. Amid the complexity of the problem and the elusiveness of a solution, one reality emerged clearly: the responsibility for law enforcement was essentially a local one, and within the local constitution, counties remained supreme.[1]

Kentucky's predilection for vigilantism and organized lawlessness originated early in statehood. The leading historian of the subject has estimated that by 1850 at least nine separate vigilante movements had manifested themselves in the Commonwealth. Civil War tensions heightened the problem as paramilitary types, primarily pro-southern in nature, began to terrorize the countryside. Ostensibly operating for the cause of high principle, many of the benighted gangs seemed more interested in common thievery than southern sovereignty, and most did not disguise their white racism. Following the war, organized aggression directed itself principally against freedmen and their allies. Composed of former Confederates and rebel sympathizers, these bands of regulators were generally identified as Ku Klux Klan by 1868. According to a leading historian of the subject, Kentucky constituted the only state outside the former Confederacy where the Klan found any significant development. Although apparently without central authority and direction, Kentucky's Klansmen reportedly inflicted as many outrages "in size, frequency, and brutality" as their counterparts elsewhere.[2]

Timidity, ineffectiveness, and even connivance characterized government response to activity of the Klan in Kentucky. Kentucky's governors claimed not to have responsibility for the suppression of the Klan and legislatures mostly studied the problem. Both rightfully placed the burden of law enforcement on county government. But so ineffectual was their response to the Klan, that the *New York Times* branded county officials as "particeps criminis." After Klansmen had preyed upon blacks in Franklin County, raping a young girl, ducking two men in a cold stream, and killing others, a special legislative committee investigated the incidents and, rather than recommending new legislation, urged county officials to enforce the law more effectively, noting their disregard in this area. When the General Assembly finally did act in 1873, it not only specifically penalized groups of masked outlaws but also provided punishments for delinquent county peace officers. Concentrated for the most part in the central and western parts of the state, Klan activity dissipated by 1875, although isolated incidents were reported as late as 1889.[3]

The disorganized state of Kentucky violence did not last long. Feuds soon replaced the Klan as a new, even more sinister form of collective action. Pitting family against family, political faction against faction, they often produced carnages rivaling those of the Civil War. Occurring mostly in the eastern part of the Commonwealth, the feuds stemmed from a variety of causes, not the least of which involved bitter family rivalries dating from the war. Widespread ignorance and poverty and a general lack of such stabilizing institutions such as well-established churches hastened and intensified the drift toward anarchy. The unwillingness or inability of county peace officers to keep the peace likewise aggravated the condition. And pervading the entire process, in the opinion of some, was the condition of deep-seated parochialism caused by Kentucky's excessive number of counties.[4]

Conflict over county offices often precipitated feuds; failure of county officers to enforce laws often perpetuated them. Breathitt County's election for county judge in 1878, for example, sparked a heated conflict between factions which had originated during the Civil War. Four months after the election, county judge J. W. Burnett led one of the factions in a pitched battle against the other in the streets of the county seat. On the following day, an unknown assailant murdered Burnett as he and his gang of "toughs" attempted to lead a member of the opposition to jail. As the battle continued to rage, the sheriff eagerly joined the fray as a "partisan," all other county officers resigned or fled, the circuit judge took a leave of absence, and none of the justices of the peace would take the deceased county judge's place. Amid this state of anarchy, Governor James B. McCreary sent in state troops to restore order, however temporarily. Breathitt County's subsequent exploits would earn it the nickname "Bloody Breathitt."[5]

In many ways the most spectacular feud of nineteenth-century Kentucky began in much the same way as had that in Breathitt County. In 1884 Republicans and Democrats of Rowan County engaged in a bitter contest over the sheriffalty, with the Republican candidate, Cook Humphrey, winning narrowly. On election night a fight broke out between Republicans and Democrats in a tavern in Morehead, the county seat, resulting in the death of a Democrat, Soloman Bradley, and the wounding of John Martin, a prominent Republican. Later in December, Martin revenged this attack by killing his assailant, Floyd Tolliver, a member of the most prominent Democratic family in the county; Martin then was placed in the Montgomery County jail to avoid retribution by the sizable Tolliver clan. Undaunted, the Tollivers falsified a court order for Martin's release to the Rowan County jail and spirited him away on a train to Morehead, despite his allegations of a setup. Unfortunately for Martin, his predictions proved accurate, for he was removed from the train before it reached its destination and murdered by the Tollivers.[6]

The murder of John Martin inaugurated a two-and-one-half-year period of skirmishes and pitched battles between the Martin-led Republicans and the Tolliver-dominated Democrats. In early 1885 members of the Martin faction ambushed and wounded Taylor Young, son of Zachery Young, Democratic county attorney and prominent member of the Tolliver faction. Shortly thereafter the Tolliver gang declared open warfare on sheriff Humphrey and his deputies, accusing him of conspiring with John Martin to kill Floyd Tolliver and plotting to jail the Tollivers en masse in order to put them out of business. In April 1885 a gunfight broke out between the two factions in the streets of Morehead, sending sheriff Humphrey into hiding and the remainder of the county officers, save the county clerk, into temporary retirement. In the summer, members of the Tolliver gang surrounded the home of John Martin's mother, flushed out Cook Humphrey (who fortunately escaped to Kansas), killed one of his deputies, and arrested two of the Martin daughters on bogus charges.

The Tollivers then arranged for Ed Pearce, a fugitive from justice, to swear falsely that Humphrey and the Martins had conspired to assassinate county attorney Young, and thereupon surrendered themselves to two justices of the peace, one of them a Tolliver partisan, for preliminary hearing, after swearing the Republican county judge off the bench. Young withdrew from the case, professing his obviously prejudicial interest in the case, and Governor J. Proctor Knott, a chagrined observer of Rowan County's anarchy, sent in the attorney general to direct the preliminary prosecution. What followed compounded the mockery. The prosecution forced Pearce to admit that his accusations against Humphrey and the Martins were false. Young then entered the case, claiming that he, not the attorney general, should be the prosecutor and forced Pearce to reaffirm his original charges. After much bickering between "prosecutors," the Republican magistrate voted to bind the Tollivers over to the grand jury, but his Democratic colleague voted to release and the defendants went free. Shortly therafter, the grand jury, packed with Tolliver allies, completed the farce by indicting Mrs. Martin for poisoning a turkey.

Although some, such as the *Louisville Courier-Journal*, called for a crackdown on Rowan County and even its abolition, the state government continued to maintain its generally hands-off posture, and the Tolliver faction continued the offensive on its beleaguered opposition. In the August elections of 1886 it secured control of county government, electing all officers save that of county judge, but that was filled by one James Stewart, whose semi-illiteracy was exceeded only by his cowardice. Early in 1887 Craig Tolliver, leader of his family's band of miscreants, was elected police judge of Morehead, thereby completing the tyranny. In June of that year, the Tollivers, pursuing their reign of terror which had driven half of Morehead and large numbers of rural residents out of the county, imprisoned Dr. Logan, a former ally, for supposedly conspiring to murder Zachery Young, and then shot two of Logan's sons in the back after arresting them as accomplices.

Boone Logan, brother of the victims, after fleeing the county in fear of his life, journeyed to Frankfort to appeal to Governor Knott for military assistance against the Tollivers. Rebuffed by Knott, who continued his ostrichlike claim that Rowan County's murderous affair was the sole responsibility of its peace officers, all of whom were Tollivers or their allies, Logan formed a group of vigilantes who launched a surprise attack on the Tolliver encampment in Morehead on June 22. In the ensuing battle, the regulators killed Craig Tolliver and many of his henchmen and proclaimed an end to the three-year war.

Undaunted by their defeat, the remnants of the Tolliver gang sent out for more men and materiel, prompting Governor Knott finally to send in state troops, who intercepted several caseloads of rifles bound for the belligerents and at least temporarily maintained order. The county and commonwealth attorneys, still alive and allied with the Tollivers, prosecuted several of the regulators for murder, but the first unbiased jury in several decades of Rowan County history acquitted them all. So outrageous had the affair become in the eyes of the legislature that it only narrowly defeated a bill which would have abolished the county.

Although its origins differed from those in Rowan and Breathitt counties, Perry County's feud of 1887-1889 made the same impact on local peace officers, who refused to act either out of fear or out of partisanship. While earlier disputes had arisen in the county over elections, the great feud erupted because of a business rivalry between the French and Eversole families, spiced by the intrigues of an Iago-like associate of the former. Fighting between factions rallying around the two families began in the summer of 1887, and by autumn of 1888 the county was in a state of anarchy, half of the residents of the county seat, Hazard, having fled. The county officials mostly favored the Eversoles and did more to disrupt than to keep the peace. At the beginning of the feud, Joe Eversole's father-in-law was county judge, and after August 1888 his brother took over the office. Both refused consistently to issue arrest warrants. Sheriff James L. Howard, another Eversole ally, refused to arrest two noted desperadoes, also part of the Eversole faction, because they were his "friends." What prisoners there were in jail frequently escaped with the connivance of the sheriff and his deputies. Grand juries, either sympathizing with lawbreakers or intimidated by them, failed to return indictments. Unable to gain access to the offices and leverage of county government, the French faction in self-defense employed a special "posse" of Breathitt County thugs. Finally and reluctantly in the fall of

1888 Governor Knott sent the state guard into the county to restore order, but as soon as the troops exited, fighting resumed. As the period of the third constitution ended, hostilities still simmered.[7]

Similar feuds occurred, sometimes more than once, in some other counties, including Bell, Owen, Garrard, Letcher, Harlan, Knott, and, of course, Pike (the famed Hatfields and the McCoys). Feuds constituted only the most sensational form of lawlessness. Ordinary crime mushroomed also in the second half of the century drawing loud complaints from politicians and citizens alike that peace officers stood idly by while thugs robbed, maimed, and murdered. Appalled by the disorder and nonenforcement, the *Courier-Journal* concluded that in some counties there was "practically no law . . . not even mob law; not even the law which in Italy and Spain relieves the vendetta of some of its most brutal features." The *New York Times* described Kentucky as the "Corsica of America."

Many attributed the feuds and lawlessness in general to an excessive number of counties and the inadequacies of their officers. "These little county organisms are storm centers from which feuds are created. . . .from which antagonisms radiate," argued Bennett H. Young, delegate to the constitutional convention of 1890-1891. In Young's opinion, many of the feuds themselves began as the result of disputes over the spoils of county office and perpetuated themselves amid the natural hostilities of closely knit communities. Echoing these charges, the *Courier-Journal* submitted that once a "county brawl" began, it inevitably encompassed large segments of typically small counties and that widespread involvement made it impossible to find an impartial jury. Others observed that county peace officers frequently became partisans themselves, noting that in one county the sheriff refused to arrest alleged criminals because he was allied with them, while the county judge only sought their imprisonment because he was their political enemy. Rare was the suggestion by W. H. Miller, delegate to the constitutional convention of 1890-1891, that more effective law enforcement required even smaller counties in order to overcome problems of time, space, and population.[8]

County officials would have found themselves at the storm center of the crime controversy regardless of the number of counties because traditionally they were the principal conservators of the peace. Together with town and city marshals and urban policemen, the sheriffs and their deputies, the county judges, the justices of the peace, the jailers, the coroners, and the constables constituted the corps of peace officers for the Commonwealth. Of these, the sheriff's position was foremost. He was the principal peace officer of the county, charged with the duty of apprehending all fugitives of justice, as well as with transporting them to and from jail and to the penitentiary or gallows if necessary. Additionally, sheriffs summoned jurors, served warrants, and attended to the numerous other duties of the chief executive officer of the county and circuit-criminal courts. Constitutionally defined as "conservators of the peace," county judges and justices of the peace acted primarily as adjudicators rather than enforcers. County judges served concurrently with justices of the peace as examining courts, having exclusive jurisdiction over homicides after 1885. The judges also shared jurisdiction with the justices over riots, routs, and breaches of the peace and after 1875 absorbed the surplus cases of misdemeanors which had been steadily building up on the dockets of circuit and criminal courts. Two justices of the peace (after 1885 only one) constituted examining courts and single justices could hear cases of minor misdemeanors. Justices were also charged with the suppression of routs, riots, and breaches of the peace and disorderly conduct, which included apprehension as well as adjudication (with the aid of a jury) and had somewhat the same task regarding vagrancy. Both county judges and justices could issue arrest warrants. Occasionally county courts, either in the person of the county judge or the court of claims, offered rewards for the apprehension of fugitives from justice.[9]

Although his duties normally concerned only the daily care of prisoners and the maintenance of the jail and other county buildings, the jailer on occasion apprehended fugitives from justice, especially escapees from jail. Coroners conducted inquests by jury into suspicious deaths and housebreakings and either arrested the "culpable" persons personally or "caused it to be done by [their] precepts." They also acted for the sheriff in cases of illness or other incapacity. Constables continued to serve the justices of the peace and sometimes assisted sheriffs and other peace officers in the apprehension of fugitives. In addition to these traditional duties, county officers were sometimes given special assignments by the legislature, such as enforcing statutes relating to game preservation, peddlers, the prohibition of prize fights, and the sale and storage of illuminating oils.[10]

Kentuckians, especially governors of the state, frequently complained of the inadequacies of law enforcement. Amid the epidemic of vigilante activity during Reconstruction, governors were quick to point out their limited powers of law enforcement and to criticize those primarily responsible, the county officers. Governor Stevenson urged county officials to enforce criminal laws more forcefully, and his successor, P. H. Leslie, charged that the "difficulty lies not in the want of penal statutes, but in their enforcement." In 1872 a special House committee blamed Ku Klux Klan outrages in Franklin County on peace officers who did little in the way of interrogating, investigating, or arresting despite the fact that "the disturbers of the public peace are well known to the public and the officers of the law." Rather than recommend new laws, the committee beseeched the sheriff and his colleagues to attend to their existing duties. A Pendleton County journalist complained in 1877 of "little effort" to apprehend the many killers that roamed the locality, and the *New York Times* ascribed Kentucky's mounting crime wave to "weak administration of law." On the eve of constitutional reform, Governor Simon B. Buckner announced that "nothing was more common than to find civil officers disregarding their plain duty, either by failure to issue proper process, or by neglecting, and even refusing, to serve process placed in their hands for execution."[11]

A gradual evolution in the office of sheriff accounted for many of the deficiencies of law enforcement. The Frankfort *Kentucky Yeoman* explained this process well in 1872:

> The old common law idea of a sheriff's relation to the people, and that which has prevailed until a comparatively recent period was that he was the peace officer of the county, and the special terror of offenders against the law. Gradually the civil branch of the sheriff's duties has been enlarged, and almost absorbs his whole time. As the collector of the revenue of the state and county he has a harassing and responsible position sufficient almost to occupy the time of one person, and is besides the executive officer of the circuit court, who executes its processes and enforces its judgment. The fees which go to make his salary come almost exclusively from this branch of his business. So that, what from the poor pay and the absence of positive law requiring him to act, the sheriff as known to us now-a-days bears altogether different relations to crime from what he did a quarter of a century ago.

Some sheriffs did their utmost to keep the peace, arresting gangs of desperadoes, apprehending "mobs of regulators," even occasionally dying in shoot-outs with fugitives. But the majority neglected their law enforcement duties even after the legislature made them more "positive" in 1873.[12]

Sheriffs were not the only county officers who failed to enforce the criminal laws effectively. Rockcastle County Democrats accused the Republican county judge of assisting an accused murderer and fellow party member to escape after he purportedly murdered a Democrat shortly before the August 1867 elections, a charge the judge hotly denied. In 1883 the Robertson county attorney attempted to have a homicide case transferred to two different justices of the peace, alleging that the two before whom the case had been filed had prejudged the dispute in favor of the defendant, and similar such examples may have prompted the General Assembly to give county judges exclusive jurisdiction over preliminary hearings of homicide cases in 1886. Richard Stanton, foremost authority on the justice of the peace in the latter nineteenth century, accused the local magistrates of almost total failure to enforce the statute prohibiting the carrying of concealed weapons, an allegation seconded by the *Kentucky Yeoman*. An Owensboro journalist found Kentucky justices very inconsistent in behavior, some "making the law a terror to evil doers" while others erred so often "on mercy's side" that they constituted "an accessory after the fact."[13]

Not all the blame for inadequate law enforcement lay with those county officers charged with investigation and apprehension. Critics accused county attorneys as well of incompetence. Too often, they argued, these officials were young and inexperienced and therefore usually bested in trials by defense counsel. Although for most of the period of the third constitution county attorneys prosecuted only misdemeanors, in 1884 the legislature required them to assist commonwealth attorneys in the prosecution of felonies. Defenders of the office cited this legislation as proof of the county attorney's worth. Commonwealth attorneys, they submitted, had too much territory to cover and too little time in which to prepare for cases. Furthermore, county attorneys understood local mores, knew witnesses, judges, and juries, and had more time to study the facts of the case. Criminal prosecution had become more effective since the local prosecutors came to the assistance of the commonwealth's attorneys. Critics countered this development by noting that families of victims of criminal defendants continued to employ private counsel to assist the prosecution, an indication that the inadequacies of public prosecutors, whether operating individually or jointly, persisted.[14]

Other officials and institutions of the law-enforcement process encountered criticism. Circuit and criminal court judges could not keep their dockets current as the number of criminal cases mounted. They were too lenient toward criminals and too fearful of their own safety, frequently refusing to hold court in counties torn by feuding. Observers also complained that judges too often granted continuances of major felony cases to the point where material witnesses became unavailable, making trials impossible and allowing dangerous criminals to go free. Defenders of prosecutors and judges countered that Kentucky's criminal code made it difficult to secure convictions. They further charged that this condition had been deliberately created by the multitude of lawyers who dominated the legislature and who wished to facilitate their criminal defense practices.[15]

The jury system likewise contained serious deficiencies. Sheriffs frequently ignored lists compiled by jury commissioners and instead relied on "professional jurymen," noted for their menial status and leniency. A reporter for the *Louisville Evening Post* in 1879 determined that many men on the Jefferson County jury list were excused peremptorily or not even summoned. Two years earlier a Nicholas County murderer, convicted of stoning a man to death, thanked his jury for sentencing him to only eleven years in prison, admitting that he believed "he deserved the extreme penalty of the law" and expressing "surprise at the light sentence."[16]

Critics also charged governors with exercising too freely their pardoning power. The *New York Times* contended that the "reckless exercise of the pardoning power by the Governor has been a direct incitement to crime." Responding to such accusations, Governor Blackburn argued in 1881 that he had pardoned many convicted criminals because of conditions in the state penitentiary. "When I came into the Executive Office there were 969 convicts in the Penitentiary, and only 780 cells, and these cells were but three feet nine inches wide, six feet three inches high, and six feet eight inches long," Blackburn stated. Noting that prisoners were "dying at a fearful rate" and vowing that the penitentiary should not be "a charnel-house," Blackburn claimed he was only being humane in liberally implementing his pardoning power. The governor also took the occasion to make a startling charge against county prosecuting attorneys, asserting that in order to inflate their own fee income, many had obtained convictions of persons who had committed only trivial crimes. In short, Blackburn contended, the fault lay not with the governor, but with conditions at the penitentiary and pressures prompted by the fee system which caused prosecutors to "hunt out the small peccadilloes . . . that they may profit by their fines and forfeitures."[17]

Kentucky's crime wave not only endangered life, limb, and property, but the state treasury as well. By statute the state absorbed most of the cost of criminal law enforcement, paying salaries and fees for commonwealth's attorneys and circuit and criminal court judges, as well as fees for witnesses, juries, and special guards and many of the fees for jailers, sheriffs, county court clerks, and county attorneys. Governor Leslie noted that in 1865 "the cost of prosecuting criminals, including jailers' fees, and rewards paid for apprehending and delivering persons charged with crime was $86,080.82, while in 1871 the amount had increased to $192,002.88. Two years later the figure had reached $234,966.46, and by 1889 the amount had soared to nearly $600,000. A substantial part of these expenditures constituted jailers' fees which were greatly enhanced by the constant delays in bringing prisoners to trial. State expenditures for county juries rose from $140,215.95 to $361,244.59 in a single three-year period (1886-1889).[18]

State officials accused county peace officers of inflating expenses by submitting fraudulent claims. Not a few justices of the peace, sheriffs, and constables staged collusive "crimes" in order to manufacture claims against the state. They would usually engage several men to commence a friendly fight in which one would sustain a minor injury, and the other would "flee" to another county, leaving word where he could be found. The county peace officer "with a guard or two" would then apprehend the "fugitive" and submit a claim for transporting a prisoner from one county to another, a trip which usually took several days. Responding to a plea from Governor Buckner, the General Assembly cracked down on fraudulent claims in a series of three statutes passed in 1880. Five years later the state auditor reported that although the new legislation had served to suppress the "more open and flagrant frauds," many county officers continued to submit unnecessarily inflated claims for the cost of apprehending and transporting fugitives.[19]

In the opinion of some, the excessive number of counties added to the financial burdens of the battle against crime. Not only did the smallness of counties multiply the conditions producing crime but it also increased the numbers of officials submitting claims whether fraudulent or legitimate. The demands of counties "on the state treasury are altogether out of proportion to population or wealth," the *Courier-Journal* editorialized in 1885. In the following year, Governor Knott demanded unsuccessfully that the legislature transfer the principal costs of law enforcement onto the counties which had become "systematic conspiracies to pillage the public treasury."[20]

Kentucky's lawlessness and the counties' inability to cope with it naturally produced growing public outrage. Franklin countians employed the customary techniques of protestation when between 1871 and 1873 they petitioned the General Assembly "for such legislation as will suppress certain disorders in said county" and held a series of meetings condemning criminal activity and urging county officers to make greater efforts to suppress it. The Pendleton County committee of safety of 1877-1879 concerned itself with both fiscal abuses of county government and its inattention to criminal law enforcement. Fayette countians held a series of meetings in the late 1860s and throughout the 1870s in response to activities of the Ku Klux Klan, although the last recorded conclave, in February 1878, adjourned sine die for want of attendance.[21]

The absence of effective law enforcement prompted other citizens to opt for more violent expressions of outrage designed to reduce the crime rate. Vigilantism, whether in the form of the Ku Klux Klan or some other organization, represented a response of citizens unable to obtain relief from the duly constituted organ of government. Although lamenting the existence of extralegal law enforcement, observers such as the Lexington *Kentucky Gazette* and the *Lexington Weekly Press* predicted a continuance of it as long as county and city peace officers were held in disrepute and citizens remained in fear of their lives. The *Gazette* even defended a mob lynching of an alleged murderer in March 1879, although the *Kentucky Yeoman* a year later condemned citizens of Boyd, Lawrence, and Carter counties for taking the law into their own hands rather than relying on county peace officers to preserve order. Organized mobs did occasionally contribute to domestic tranquillity, such as the Nicholas County regulators who drove from the county a band of outlaws and horse thieves in 1876-1877, but many behaved like the Ku Klux Klan which in the name of law and order fashioned its own brand of lawlessness.[22]

While some citizens protested or regulated or both, others groped for more rational and effective ways to subdue Kentucky's crime. Governor Preston H. Leslie called for greater penalties against peace officers who failed to enforce the law, and the legislature responded in kind in 1873. But the statute accomplished little, and Governor Buckner renewed the call for stiffer penalties for official nonfeasance in 1889. Buckner even advocated creation of a state department of justice, under the control of the attorney general, which could compel local prosecuting officers to discharge their duty. He also suggested that the legislature impeach and remove all incompetent judges from office.[23]

Some recommended that the General Assembly enhance the governor's authority to quash local lawlessness by use of the state guard. County officers seemed to favor such a course as they frequently and often unsuccessfully sought military assistance from the statehouse. But governors themselves rejected this proposal, arguing that the primary responsibility for law enforcement should continue to rest with local officials. Habitual reliance on state troops would cause Kentucky's citizenry to lose confidence in civil government and threaten the "principles of free government," Governor Buckner submitted. Sheriffs would neglect their law enforcement duties, rely unduly on the military, and the state would be forced to maintain an army at considerable expense. If governors eschewed a greater role for themselves in law enforcement, they did recognize that the traditional weapons available to local peace officers were inadequate. Governor Leslie contended in 1872 that the *posse comitatus*, "the only reliance of the civil officer for aid in pursuing and arresting offenders," could not cope with well-drilled bands of criminals. "The posse are neither drilled nor armed, and hence not prepared to encounter the offenders." Even more cumbersome, he added, was the militia which could never be assembled in time to confront the enemy. At best, bands of criminals simply went into hiding when the militia appeared, only to continue their pillaging as soon as the soldiers were withdrawn.[24]

Faced with mounting crime, peace officers who could not keep the peace, regulators who did not regulate, and governors who seldom sent in state troops, some counties flirted with the concept of a professional county police force to supplement if not supplant the sheriff, his deputies, and the posse. The first requests received by the General Assembly to create special county police systems involved simply authorizations to empower "all persons" to arrest alleged poachers and illegal berrypickers. Civil War pillaging prompted the Lincoln and Hart county courts to secure legislation authorizing them to employ special police forces to guard against outlaws and guerrillas, but there is no evidence that either county implemented these statutes.[25]

Following the war, several counties secured special legislation permitting them to establish county police forces. At first approaching the problem in piecemeal fashion by allowing each precinct to vote on the question of its own police force,

Jefferson County ultimately secured legislation in 1874 allowing the creation of a countywide organization. But the county court never implemented the law and secured its repeal in 1876. Throughout the remainder of the period of the third constitution the county court occasionally appointed patrolmen, but usually only for special events, such as horse races, and always at the expense of those directly benefiting from the appointment. The Jefferson County Court so acted under a statute permitting any county court to appoint patrolmen to assist in law enforcement (although originally counties used patrols to control slaves). An examination of the order books of twenty other counties reveals that none of them established permanent patrols during the period of the third constitution, and only a few appointed patrolmen for special events such as fairs and horse races.[26]

Fayette County grappled with the concept of a county police force for over twenty years before finally deciding not to establish one. In 1867 the General Assembly authorized the county court to appoint "one chief of police . . . and not more than three policemen for each election district . . . outside the city of Lexington." But the court did not implement the statute, and in May 1876 a group of county residents petitioned the county court for the creation of a "county detective force to render their houses and property . . . more secure than they have been for a number of years." The petitioners even expressed a willingness to absorb a tax increase, believing that a fall in the crime rate would create savings in the long run. But the court of claims refused to establish a detective force, apparently fearful that it would evolve into a band of "secret police." The clamor and lawlessness persisted, and in December 1877 the *Gazette* editorialized in favor of a county police force. Claiming that the city of Lexington maintained an effective constabulary which secured the lives and property of its residents, the newspaper contended that outlaws burglarized the houses of countians "with impunity." The newspaper urged its readers to pressure the county court into action.[27]

Perhaps in response to this agitation, the legislature enacted in late February 1878 still another statute permitting the county judge to authorize the sheriff to appoint a detective force of no more than five men. Empowered to hire, discipline, and control the force and to keep "it constantly engaged in efforts to discover and bring to justice against the law of every grade," the sheriff had to confer regularly with the county attorney and court of claims. Within fifteen days of the creation of such a force, the county judge had to obtain approval of the court of claims, which had the power to set the rate of pay. Despite statutory authority, the county court refused once more to create a county police force, and Fayette County continued to rely on its traditional constabulary for protection against crime.[28]

In 1886 the legislature attempted yet again to provide better police protection for certain rural residents of Fayette, Kenton, and Campbell counties. It authorized specially created police districts of Lexington, Covington, and Newport to provide protection for designated suburban areas if taxpayers owning a majority of the assessed land so petitioned their county courts. If petitioned for police protection, the police districts could (and certainly would) require the county courts to tax the suburban residents in order to pay for their share of the policing. There is no evidence that any of the suburban areas filed such petitions with their county courts. When in 1890 the General Assembly required the Fayette County Court to tax residents of the Woodlands suburb of Lexington so that they might have city police protection, the justices simply referred the question to its committee on ways and means and filed its report without further action.[29]

Fayette County's defiance and Kenton and Campbell counties' unwillingness to use more sophisticated urban police protection represent a curious paradox in the history of Kentucky's local constitution in the nineteenth century. Politicians, journalists, and citizens continuously complained about the inadequacies of county law enforcement, but refused to tax themselves in order to provide better service. Such inconsistency characterized efforts to reform county road administration and generally undermined other attempts to modernize the institutions of local government.

6.
COURT DAY

County court day, one Monday a month devoted primarily to court business, by mid-century had evolved into an occasion with emphasis on activities of all kinds. By the end of the Civil War, the judicial-governmental nature of the event had so diminished that in some cases it went practically unnoticed. Thus the day on which the county judge and justices of the peace would come to the seat of government to do the county's business had given way to a day on which farmers and vendors sold their wares, politicians made speeches, and local citizens gossiped, imbibed, and sometimes brawled.[1]

In the Bluegrass section of the Commonwealth, court day coincided with stock sale day. Apparently originating in Bourbon County in 1829 and held there exclusively for several years, county livestock sales were major attractions at the postbellum central Kentucky court days. April was the "great cattle court" in most of the Bluegrass counties, with postwar sales flourishing in such counties as Scott, Woodford, Clark, Franklin, Fayette, and Bourbon. Winchester in Clark County prided itself as the "livest [sic] town in Kentucky" on stock day, Scott County claimed it was becoming "one of the best stock markets" in Kentucky, while Woodford County usually reported large attendances and sales. Famed Kentucky author James Lane Allen went so far as to characterize central Kentucky's court-stock days as collectively the "great stockmarket of the West."[2]

Despite Allen's claims, not every county court livestock sale enjoyed booming sales. Observers cautioned Clark County stockmen to hold their stock back in the fall of 1879 rather than add to the severe market glut which already existed. In June 1880 the Lexington *Kentucky Gazette* reported that sales in Bourbon County, whose county seat once literally overflowed with livestock on sale days, were declining because of steadily diminishing numbers of grazing animals. Five years later Fayette County's Chamber of Commerce stewed openly about the declining sales of its stock market.[3]

Fayette County's problems stemmed in part from a controversy which had been simmering for years over whether stock sales should be allowed in the public square or transferred to the suburbs, a question that plagued other counties in lesser degrees. Long boasting one of the most active court days in Kentucky, Fayette County's stock sales rivaled that of Bourbon County's in importance. In early 1853 a local newspaper reported that Lexington was "generally full of people on every county court day" and that one auctioneer alone at February court sold nearly $15,000 worth of property. Four years later another paper indicated that people continued to throng into the Bluegrass capital and that the same auctioneer had sold more than three times as much livestock, slaves, and land as he had four years earlier. If anything, crowds of people and herds of livestock increased after the war, further filling the coffers of the vendors and barkers of the public square. By war's end, what had been a pleasant social and business occasion was becoming a nuisance. Crowds of people and livestock, "loads of shingles and clapboards and baskets and watermelons and lumber" converted the public square and its environs into a scene of animated chaos on court day. Normal traffic in town became impossible, and turnpikes stuffed with herds of livestock being driven to market afforded no more accessiblity. When it rained, streets became quagmires and the "nuisance," a calamity. The sounds of thousands of people and livestock, hundreds of wagons, and scores of auctioneers and other vendors amounted to almost a deafening roar. It amazed some that Fayette countians tolerated these spectacles, and one cynic speculated that court day remained essential to keep "people from thinking that Lexington is a little country town."[4]

The livestock accounted for most of the growing complaints about Fayette County court day. They produced a stench that allegedly caused "a strong, well man" to vomit as he walked the streets, an odor that hung over Lexington throughout the summer and permeated "not only the stores but the dry goods on the shelves." Some argued that the presence of so many animals in so small a space constituted a threat to the community's health and certainly the residue of their visitation involved expensive cleanup. A clamor soon arose for better regulation of the sales. Some urged livery stable keepers to provide more ample accommodations for "country men." Others suggested that the city police regulate traffic "at the head of Cheapside," the principal avenue of livestock traffic. Still others proposed a designated route for incoming and outgoing herds rather than leaving it to chance. And most observers demanded pens or pounds for the animals as a way to curb their tendency to roam free. The most extreme critics demanded that the sales be held on Saturdays or be moved entirely out of the central city into the suburbs.[5]

Proposals to move the sales to the outskirts of town created a classic dilemma for city merchants. While most detested the "peculiar and pungent ammonia of county court day," they disliked even more the prospect of declining sales which might result from the transfer of large crowds to places remote from their places of business. Reluctantly in early 1870, they agreed to a temporary experiment of moving the auctions from Cheapside in the public square to the edge of town, but almost immediately found the change undesirable and together with disgruntled stockmen, who boycotted the new location, successfully petitioned the city fathers for a restoration of the old system. Nonetheless agitation for a permanent removal continued throughout the 1870s as indignation against the "cattle plague" mounted. Some demanded that the streets be cleared of cattle by early afternoon and that stockmen be taxed to pay for cleaning of the streets. In April 1879 stockmen, merchants, and city officials met at the courthouse to discuss the question of permanent removal of stock sales to the edge of town. The heated debate turned principally on the impact on the business of downtown merchants and the question of whether the animals constituted a health hazard. Despite denials of unhealthiness, predictions of economic disaster in the inner city, and suggestions that suburbanites would oppose stockyards in their neighborhoods, city officials ordained the move shortly after the April meeting.[6]

By ordinance the city fathers outlawed the selling "by public auction [of] any loose animal on any street, alley, or public highway within the city of Lexington or [the exposing] for sale thereon any animals in droves, herds, or flocks." While this would seem to have applied to horses and mules, Lexingtonians complained nearly ten years later that only cattle and hogs were affected by the law. Yet the general problem abated as did Cheapside sales, and the merchants there periodically grumbled and petitioned the city council for a revocation of the stock sales ordinance. But the law remained on the books throughout the rest of the period of the third constitution; and while livestock sales in Fayette County declined in the 1880s, the Lexington Chamber of Commerce voted against recommending the repeal of the ordinance and attributed the losses to other factors.[7]

Court day also attracted horsemen whether it be the simple farmer who wished to swap with a colleague or the Bluegrass aristocrat who wished to race, exhibit, and perhaps buy and sell horses. Fayette and Bourbon counties boasted the largest horse shows featuring exhibitions of "fine blooded stallions," especially the world's greatest trotters. Held at April court, formal racing sometimes formed part of the festivities. From the beginning, organizers of Fayette County's horse show avoided congesting downtown Lexington by holding their event in the city's suburbs. At first attracting horsemen from only the Bluegrass region, by the postwar period the event drew visitors from all parts of the United States. By that time also, the show featured mostly Standardbreds, the owners of Thoroughbreds preferring to display their stock at private auctions and races. Owners, not riders, dominated the nineteenth-century shows, emphasizing the speed, shape, style, and action of their horses. At the show many breeders decided upon mates for their mares and observed exhibitions of the fastest trotters in trial heats. By the early twentieth century the horse shows of most counties had faded into oblivion, but Fayette County's survived and prospered for another two decades before it, too, expired (to be revived in 1937 in a slightly different form).[8]

Court day represented a grand occasion for the barterer as well as the vendor, and horses constituted the basic object of the swap. In an age when man depended on the horse as his basic form of transportation and Kentucky prided herself on possessing the finest horses in the world, it was perhaps natural that court-day attendants would spend some time attempting to trade for a superior steed. Often swaps involved only the animals themselves, but just as often added inducements were needed, ranging from only a few dollars or a plug of tobacco to several hundred dollars. If this month's swap proved disappointing, there was always next month's court day at which to redeem oneself. Horses represented not the only items of barter. As the century matured, hand weapons, especially knives and guns, became increasingly popular items of exchange.[9]

Stockmen and horse breeders were not the only ones conducting business on court day. Peddlers and drummers of all types, including patent medicine men, lightning rod salesmen, bookmen, and machine men, flourished amid the usually large crowds of the day. The auctioneer, who figured so prominently in livestock sales, also sold slaves (before 1865), rural acreages, town lots, and all types of personal property. Town merchants offered special discounts for the day, and local craftsmen offered to sell such products as baskets and copperware. Lumbermen did a lively business from their huge stacks of wood, shingles, and clapboards, often piled in the routes of pedestrians. Local cooks proudly displayed a variety of prepared foods, including pies, cakes, corn dishes, and hot-brushes.[10]

While not all the month's business was conducted on court day, certainly much of it was. The financial community used the day to conclude a large portion of its transactions. Financiers bought and sold stocks, mostly in turnpike companies, railroads, and banks; money men bought and sold negotiable paper; and stockholders met and voted on major policy questions. So ingrained was the dependence of money men on court day that the Court of Appeals ruled that foreclosure sales were valid even though not held on the traditional Monday.[11]

In an era when most people lived on farms, worked long days, and were offered little in the way of organized, commercial leisure, court day also constituted a major social event. Nineteenth-century Kentuckians delighted in social gatherings—horse races, burgoos, barbecues, agricultural fairs, political meetings—and court day took on an appearance similar to all these affairs, even encompassing some of them. Even if they had nothing to buy or sell, country folk normally came to the county seat to enjoy the festivities at hand, as is evidenced by reports that crowded court days occasionally produced disappointing sales figures. It was essential for the well-being of the average Kentuckian to be able to press the flesh, exchange formal greetings, swap a few lies, learn the latest gossip, and banter over several glasses of punch. Such socializing became mostly a man's game as the teeming crowds of court day and the herds of livestock kept women away or drove them into stores. As with most of the other events, democracy characterized court-day socializing, with aristocrat and commoner easily exchanging pleasantries. Perhaps the Kentuckian's love of titles encouraged the leveling process. It was commonplace for virtually all white adult males to be addressed as "colonel" or "squire." A bemused correspondent to the *New York Times* following the Civil War marveled at his rapid advancement in military rank during court day; beginning as a lowly major, he ended the day as a general. Titled gentlemen so abounded at the gathering that the correspondent concluded it would be far easier to find "John Smith in New York City" than "Squire or Judge Somebody in the crowd." He noted also that a man's social position increased with the amount of bourbon whiskey he consumed and that "copper lightning awakens 'the best blood' pride" in Kentuckians, but with northerners the "dead were dead."[12]

Court day was not entirely dominated by men. Church ladies found court days especially suitable for public dinners designed to raise funds for the benefit of their respective parishes. In February 1873, for instance, the ladies of the First Presbyterian Church of Lexington announced in a local newspaper that they wished all their rural neighbors to remember they could "get a good dinner without detention . . . in Mr. Long's building on the corner of Cheapside and Short Street," while the ladies of the Baptist Church of the same town sponsored "an elegant dinner" at the April court of the same year. Women and children could sometimes seek refuge from brawling, drunken men and smelly cows by attending a circus which occasionally enlivened the monthly meetings.[13]

Court day also represented an occasion convenient for athletic competition and sporting events of all types. In addition to horse racing, athletic contests included sledgehammer throwing, bar heaving, foot racing, and cock fighting. Fighting constituted by far the most popular human sport. Although spontaneous fights occurred frequently, the most popular affairs were staged and involved "champions" from various parts of the county. Bystanders formed makeshift rings and the contestants fought until one of them could no longer resist. At first, these confrontations encompassed all parts of the body, but eventually they resembled crude boxing matches. By statute, county officials could stop such events and arrest the participants, but they seldom did. Sometimes contests involved more than two contestants, taking the form of drunken brawls or even stabbings or shootings. Initially drinking was very public, with many storekeepers maintaining supplies for their customers, but after the war sources of whiskey were usually confined to taverns, tippling houses, and personal flasks. Although some have asserted that consumption likewise receded after 1865, the evidence suggests otherwise, with some reports marveling at the absence of drunkenness and others noting it existed freely.[14]

For politicians, county court day constituted a prime opportunity for rallying, speechmaking, and buttonholing. Court day crowds expected and enjoyed the inevitable speechmaking, whose occurrences were so regular and regulated that they became almost like tournaments. Speechmaking took various forms, sometimes as debates, sometimes as straight stump speaking, and sometimes as round robins among various party favorites. Seldom was the event as spontaneous as it appeared, for the careful candidate had sent his agents into the field long before the occasion of his public pronouncements. Whether running for United States senator, assisting in a presidential campaign, or seeking a local office, the politically ambitious could find a ready audience among the teeming court day crowds. The planning of John Williams, candidate for United States Senate in 1876 was typical. Striving to take advantage of a large crowd at the Gallatin County court day on Monday, October 16, 1876, Williams wrote Roderick Perry, local political leader and a Democratic presidential elector, to post him for a speech at the county seat and get him "as big a crowd as possible." Throughout the period, political leaders convoked party meetings, nominating conventions, rallies, and barbecues on court day, and during the Civil War they exchanged news about battles and strategy. All in all, court day inevitably promised to be a grand political occasion.[15]

Court day was a special day for blacks as well as whites. In days of involuntary servitude most public slave auctions took place on court day, although the practice was not without its detractors. Some found the public sale of slaves to be obnoxious, especially when families were divided, and many owners preferred to sell their stock privately. Slavery itself prompted court day meetings, some to protest the institution, but most to defend it. Emancipation did not end the presence of blacks at court day and only slightly elevated their station on these occasions. James Lane Allen alleged derisively that blacks flocked to court day only to mimic their white employers, since they had nothing to sell nor money to buy. Local observers castigated their supposed cockiness, but out-of-state visitors noted the ease with which they mingled with the crowds and applauded their humility.[16]

The intense competition between county court days further emphasizes intercounty economic rivalries and the essential parochialism of nineteenth-century Kentucky. Bluegrass counties directed most of their envy at Bourbon County, whose local pride and boastfulness made many forget that Fayette's day constituted the most successful economic enterprise of the area. Fayette countians encouraged competition with Bourbon, whose citizens they too regarded as braggarts and chauvinists. Proclaiming that "the Bourbonites disparage everybody and everything outside of their own bounds, and are accepted for what they vaunt themselves more than for what they are really worth," the *Kentucky Gazette* urged Bourbon's "modest neighbors to assert the position to which they are entitled." Responding to a piece of Bourbon County braggadocio printed in the *Louisville Courier*, the *Cynthiana News* asserted that the Paris people were actually jealous of Harrison County and that such envy was well founded as Cynthiana excelled in every way except for numbers of "long-eared animals . . . both of quadrupeds and bipeds." Some years later the *News* urged Harrison countians to combat Bourbon's superiority in four-legged animals by establishing their own court day livestock market. "It will be better for the merchant, tradesman, the people, and everybody to spend our money at home and have them spend theirs with us," the paper concluded. Harrison was not the only county to found a livestock market in an effort to bolster her court day and economic niche. Jessamine County stockmen formed a County Stock Association in March 1869 with such a purpose in mind, and by June 1870 the new market was flourishing, having drawn the largest crowd to Nicholasville in the town's history.[17]

In areas of strong competition, scheduling of court days represented a vital element in preserving a strong county economy. The problem was especially acute in Harrison County, whose court day was on the same Monday as Fayette's, Grant's, and Nicholas's. Initially when the *Cynthiana News* suggested that the day be changed to another Monday to avoid conflict, "many persons . . . hooted and shouted at the proposition," but ultimately the idea prevailed and the local representative obtained special legislation altering the meeting date. The *News* soon thereafter proudly reported that court day crowds were at an all-time high. Other counties adopted similar strategies. Woodford and Franklin changed their meeting days to avoid clashes with Scott and Fayette, but when Jessamine changed hers she began losing sales to Clark and Fayette counties.[18]

Although most of our emphasis has been upon Bluegrass counties and their neighbors because of the nature of the sources, court days constituted major events in most, if not all, of nineteenth-century Kentucky's counties. Whether or not court day was unique to Kentucky as some claimed, it cannot be denied that the meetings of the Commonwealth's most prosperous counties, such as Bourbon's, attracted visitors from all parts of the state. In most counties the allure of court day remained fairly constant throughout most of the period of the third constitution, with some variations in the size of the crowds over a year's time. Occasional flu epidemics, sporadic occurrences of the dreaded cholera, inclement weather, and the turmoil of the Civil War kept attendance down in certain counties, but usually people resumed their old habits when normalcy returned. Rare predictions that county court day was in danger of dying out proved ill founded as in Lincoln County where the local newspaper in December 1874 forecast its decline and demise but eleven years later reported record court day crowds. Even during the war large numbers of residents appeared if some semblance of security prevailed.[19]

The advent of the automobile as the basic form of American transportation signaled the decline and fall of court day as a fundamental institution of Kentucky business and social life. Naturally this process developed more rapidly in some counties than in others. In the metropolitan centers of Louisville and Covington, court day began declining even before the introduction of the automobile; in counties with sophisticated highway systems permitting easy access to county seats, the evolution began in the early twentieth century and was in full sway following World War I. By 1928 a columnist for the *Courier-Journal* could report that "only in the more remote localities does county court day retain the semblance of its one-time prestige as an event in the community," although an historian of Fayette County wrote one year later that court day "was only recently abandoned in Lexington." Yet the tradition persisted in many mountain counties for at least a decade longer. In 1940 another columnist for the *Courier-Journal* described a rural county's court day in terms reminiscent of nineteenth-century portraits. A fat peddler used ventriloquism to sell pocket knives; another in the guise of an Indian chief puffed the healing qualities of his liquid corn remover and finally persuaded an onlooking farmer to remove his shoes and socks for a free demonstration. Soon the chief sold dozens of bottles. On the other side of the courtyard, boys and men engaged in jumping and wrestling contests, and amid the competition a fistfight erupted. Nearby a blind pauper played the fiddle in return for loose change deposited in a tin cup. Annoyed by the noise, the spraying tobacco juice, and pushing crowds, wives urged their husbands into the courthouse to attend to their legal business or to the solitude of home. As late as 1950 Wolfe County court day survived, retaining its mule and horse swapping as well as peddling and politicking. Twenty years later only a few counties observed court day regularly, and then only once a year and without connection to the meeting of the county court.[20]

7.
THE RAILROAD BINGE

No subject more clearly demonstrates the parochialism of nineteenth-century Kentucky and the unique position of her counties than that of internal improvements during the period of the third state constitution. Before 1851 counties constituted only one of several principal sources of investment for turnpikes and other transportation ventures. After this date counties became the main impetus for such enterprises which by then included a far more exciting and expensive proposition—the railroad. Because of the great risks involved, the private investor, at least in several early ventures, continued to be a secondary source of funds. (In early 1851, when Fayette countians proposed a $600,000 railroad subscription, only one private investor subscribed.) State government, which during the middle years of the second constitution had contributed nearly $5 million to internal improvements, bowed out almost entirely after 1851.

Reflecting disenchantment over poor returns from state investments in turnpike projects, the constitution framers of 1850 required the legislature to secure popular approval of all indebtedness over $500,000 and to liquidate debts within thirty years. The opposition of state lawmakers to participation in transportation ventures actually increased during the period of the third constitution. By 1870 most of the richer counties had invested heavily in their own pet schemes and wanted no part of statewide endeavors. And in some of the most prosperous counties such as Fayette, railroad supporters from the outset favored county over state assistance because the latter would only benefit so-called pauper counties at the expense of self-sustaining ones. Thus as time passed, there was an increasingly large bloc of legislative votes against state aid, despite frequent demands for assistance. So uninterested did legislators become in internal improvements that in 1871 they passed laws requiring the state to sell its nearly $3 million worth of turnpike stock, although they repealed the statutes in the following year.[1]

The nonexistence of state funds, the inadequacy of private funds, and the splendor of the iron horse stimulated the local units of the constitution to support railroad ventures with a devotion that outweighed any other expenditure. Although two railroads had been completed and two others authorized before the third constitution went into effect, railroading in Kentucky did not begin in earnest until the 1850s. At the beginning of the decade there was less than 100 miles of track; by 1890 over 2,500 miles existed. Midway in the period, it was estimated that counties, cities, and towns had an outstanding railroad debt of nearly $14 million.[2]

But impressive as these figures are, progress was not made without much frustration and failure, litigation and confrontation. Early in the era, opponents sought court injunctions and judgments prohibiting public assistance to railroads and other internal improvements on the grounds that such aid was unconstitutional. The most famous and influential of these cases involved efforts of Mason County citizens to prevent county contributions to the Maysville & Lexington Railroad. In February 1851, pursuant to legislation and county court authorization, Mason County voters endorsed a $150,000 subscription to the railroad stock. Shortly thereafter Jacob Slack and 150 other citizens owning property of more than one-tenth of the entire taxable property of the county sought to prevent the subscription by a court ruling that county tax support of railroads was unconstitutional. The litigation worked its way to the Court of Appeals, which ruled early in 1852 that the taxation was valid. While basing its decision principally upon the Constitution of 1799, the tribunal implied that the new frame of government likewise allowed such expenditures and no subsequent case ever reversed this precedent.[3]

Undaunted by legal attacks, railroad promoters created during the period of the third state constitution an almost carnival atmosphere. Meetings and conventions, often called by officers and directors of railroad companies, enticed local citizens to learn the fantastic benefits of the new revolutionary form of transportation. Newspaper editorials and advertisements extolled its virtues. Court day orators echoed the calls for a network of tracks to join the state's principal communities with one another. Sometimes conclaves endorsed county subscriptions to specific railroads; other times, they simply advocated aid to railroads as a general proposition. But never did oratory or railroad meetings legally bind counties to subscriptions; they simply promoted. Binding subscriptions (if subscriptions were ever binding) emanated from a more complex procedure.[4]

Not even the most zealous of railroad promoters suggested that counties could subscribe to railroad stocks without specific legislative approval. As with almost all its other "extraordinary" business, county courts inevitably secured specific legislative authorization before investing in railroads. Normally such statutes required county courts to secure voter approval before subscriptions could be made. Sometimes railroads themselves were permitted to petition county courts to hold elections, and not infrequently courts were then required to hold such elections, although sometimes they were given a right of refusal. Statutes also varied on the question of who was to endorse a proposed subscription. Some acts specified a majority of votes cast, while others called for a majority of qualified voters. Usually one did not have to be a property holder or taxpayer to vote, although detractors of county railroad investment contended otherwise. If voters approved a subscription, the county court customarily bought the stock of the railroad, usually by issuing its bonds to the company, which in turn sold the bonds to investors. Occasionally only parts of counties voted on subscriptions, but this was a rarity.[5]

The glamour of railroads, the vision of bonanza times, and the lack of central planning and control prompted some counties and cities to combat one another over the location of prospective roads or to meddle in the subscription elections of neighbors. Chief among these protagonists was Louisville, Kentucky's largest city and its most successful and important railroad hub. Louisville sought not only to enhance her own position but also to undercut that of her chief rival, Lexington. As early as 1851 Louisvillians were reportedly encouraging "disaffected persons" in Boyle County to oppose a possible route to Lexington and to favor one to Frankfort. Three years later critics accused the River City of harboring jealousies against the proposed Nashville & Cincinnati Railroad for fear that Lexington would become the southern focal point of a vast northern system of railroads. Shortly after the Civil War, agents of the Louisville & Nashville, the most successful railroad in Louisville and statewide, stalled legislative approval of the Cincinnati Southern, which threatened to enhance Fayette County at its expense, and simultaneously worked to defeat Clark County's proposed subscription to the Elizabethtown, Lexington & Big Sandy Railroad, another potential central Kentucky rival. Late in the period, the L & N continued its campaign of self-protection, actively opposing Woodford County's proposed subscription to the Versailles & Midway Railroad in 1885 and sending one of its agents with plenty of "boodle" to scotch Mercer County's flirtation with the rival Louisville & Southern Railroad.[6]

Other cities, counties, and parts of counties engaged in similar warfare. Lexington, while fighting Louisville on her western flank, reportedly undermined Bourbon County on her right by helping to secure defeat of its proposed subscription to the Paris & Maysville Railroad in 1870. Much of the other conflict concerned prospective routes. In 1851 Danville opposed location of the Lexington & Danville through Harrodsburg because it would create the possibility of extending the road to Nashville and thus create a potential rivalry. In the same year, Franklin County sent a delegation to persuade Mercer County to build a railroad to Frankfort rather than Lexington, while in 1872 Clark countians campaigned to have the Frankfort, Paris & Big Sandy Railroad built through Mount Sterling rather than Owingsville. In 1869 a number of counties send their judges to Cincinnati to lobby over the location of her planned railroad south, and in Fayette County certain property owners pledged money to the railroad to ensure location through Lexington. Residents of Fayette County's North Middleton Precinct were incensed when in 1851 backers of the Maysville & Lexington Railroad, the most prominent of which was Fayette County itself, opted for a route through Paris instead of their own precinct. Rivalries also broke out between railroads over access to county investment funds. Conflict that began in 1851 between the Lexington & Maysville Railroad and the Lexington & Covington Railroad over joint use of a Lexington terminal and track between Lexington and Paris eventually involved efforts by both to exclude the other from Fayette County funds. Compromise and insolvency eventually tempered the confrontation. Twenty years later the Lexington & Maysville Railroad and the Frankfort, Paris & Big Sandy Railroad unsuccessfully sought to exclude each other from Bourbon County's subscription.[7]

If counties and railroads fought among themselves over stock subscriptions, so did town and country. Usually urban areas favored, while rural areas generally opposed, public financing of railroad construction. Rare was the Lexingtonian who urged in November 1858 that his city government not invest in a local railroad project because it would benefit the county more than the city. City voters were remarkably enthusiastic about railroads considering that they were often taxed twice as residents of two separate local governments, city and county, each making stock subscriptions. Sample votes in Fayette, Scott, and Bourbon counties indicate that city voters usually endorsed most railroad subscriptions by margins of from two to one to five to one, while county voters invariably opposed such schemes by ratios of from two to one to seven to one. The most sensational episode of city-county friction over railroad investment occurred in Bourbon County following the Civil War. Emboldened by their county judge's intransigence, Bourbon County justices of the peace refused by a vote of eleven to three to submit to the voters a stock subscription proposition of the Frankfort, Paris & Big Sandy Railroad. Detractors of the county court were quick to point out that the three justices who supported submission were all from Paris and represented more voters than the other eleven rural magistrates. After much agitation, supporters of the railroad secured from the legislature an amendment to the railroad's charter requiring the county court to submit the question to the voters. Although the urban vote narrowly carried the question, resentment was so great against the tactics of victory that the legislature required that all future Boubon County subscriptions have the separate endorsement of voters residing outside of the Paris city limits. Symbolic of the endless turmoil which surrounded most railroad questions, Paris residents challenged the statute in the Court of Appeals, which upheld its validity. Toward the end of the period, separate voting also occurred in Fayette County-Lexington railroad subscription referenda.[8]

Most county railroad subscription elections produced debate about the merits of public investment. Proponents of public aid were almost euphoric at times. "The locomotive . . . has become the universal bond of commerce and manufactures, and is the most powerful social, political, and moral agent the world has ever seen," claimed a correspondent to the *Paris True Kentuckian*, writing in support of the Maysville & Big Sandy Railroad. To the *Frankfort Commonwealth* the dawn of the railroad age presented to Kentucky "a prospect of trade, wealth and general prosperity . . . such as it delights the heart to contemplate."

Fayette County newspapers predicted that their community would become the "focal point of railroads in Kentucky" complete with iron foundries and textile mills; its population would increase sevenfold within a short time. Railroad supporters in depressed eastern Kentucky argued that the new transportation would eradicate poverty and permit the exploitation of the area's rich timber and mineral supplies. "Build railroads through the counties of Kentucky and you will never hear of 'pauper counties' again," reported the *Mt. Sterling Democrat*.[9]

Other supporters emphasized more specific economic benefits such as cheaper fuel and transportation costs as well as an enlarged marketplace for agricultural products; and, at least early in the period, supporters envisioned railroad profits more than defraying interest costs. After the Civil War, faced with what many believed to be a monopoly, proponents foresaw proposed new lines offering needed competition and reduced rates.[10]

A strong strain of fatalism permeated much of the pro-railroad debate. Supporters worried aloud about the consequences of not joining the railroad orgy. "We assume it as indispensable that we must adopt the railroads; for otherwise we must inevitably decline in prosperity and power, in a fruitless rivalry with enterprising neighbors on all sides of us, who are constructing them with an energy and comprehensiveness of policy challenging the highest administration," lamented a pamphleteer in behalf of Mason County's proposed subscription to the Maysville & Lexington Railroad. Others reiterated this theme of keeping pace with the competition. The Lexington *Kentucky Statesman* declared in 1851 that Kentucky had lagged behind its railroad-building neighbors too long. The same paper seemed never to be satisfied with the progress of Lexington and Fayette. In 1851 it predicted that Lexington would become "one of the first cities of the West," but in 1860 she had yet to "wake up from her Rip Van Winkle sleep." Matters had not improved by 1867 as Lexington was almost "a finished town."[11]

Initially opponents of county financing of railroads based their reservations on gloomy glances into the future. In time, as some railroads burgeoned but many others collapsed, skeptics grounded their complaints on history. Early detractors forecast staggering taxes, ruinous competition with surrounding counties, and incompetent railroad management. Post-Civil War critics decried the immunity of railroads from county taxation and pointed to the financial instability of most companies. Others denounced debt manipulation by railroad speculators, which allowed them to swallow up whole companies at the expense of the public investment and predicted like consequences for future endeavors. To some there were too many railroads already, and to others a few railroads were on the verge of monopolizing the nation's transportation. As the result of the relative success of a handful of companies, opponents of county subscription argued that private funds were adequate to finance future construction. For still others, economic conditions were never certain enough to permit major commitments of funds.[12]

Shortly after the Civil War, when the railroad binge revived, critics began revitalizing and expanding their objections to public financing which had been voiced by earlier detractors. It was wrong, they charged, for a majority to compel a minority to invest through taxation in a private enterprise. Such submission struck "a fatal blow at the very foundation of social order and equitable government." As if monolithic, these majorities became "little better than individual despotisms." Enfranchisement of the freedmen, whose voting participation was inevitably characterized as pro-railroad in herdlike fashion, made public subscription even more obnoxious. Furthermore, vote-buying often tainted subscription referenda. Taxation should be restricted to public uses. If this was not valid constitutional doctrine then it should be made so by constitutional amendment.[13]

For the most part, critics of railroads and their public financing proved accurate in their forecasts of disaster. Few enterprises proved profitable. Many were never built, and those which were usually underwent at least one reorganization in bankruptcy. Regardless of the outcome, counties frequently lost their investment and were left with staggering debts. A few examples will illustrate the problem.

In 1851 Fayette County and its neighbors attempted to launch four railroads, all of which either were not completed or resulted in financial failures for their original public investors. On March 26, 1851, after much debate for and against the proposition, Fayette County voted overwhelmingly to subscribe $200,000 each to the Lexington & Danville and to the Maysville & Lexington railroads. Shortly thereafter it subscribed another $200,000 to the Covington & Lexington Railroad. Even though Jessamine and Boyle counties likewise endorsed subscriptions and the three public stockholders had paid in over $200,000, the Danville Railroad was on the verge of collapse in late 1854. Despite the initial lack of success, more funds were raised from the three counties and construction of the line began in earnest. Yet by mid-1858 the track had been laid only from Lexington to Nicholasville with more funds needed for further construction. Late that same year, the three counties refused to purchase the railroad at a foreclosure sale despite legislative authorization, and the company passed forever into the hands of private speculators. The line was not finally completed until after the period of the third constitution.[14]

The Maysville and Covington lines suffered similar fates. Both were sold in foreclosure to railroad speculator R. B. Bowler in 1858 and 1859, thereby eliminating the interest of Fayette, Mason, and Bourbon counties, the principal shareholders. The investment in the Maysville road alone approached $1 million. Both roads became part of the Kentucky Central Railroad Company after the Civil War, the Maysville route having been completed only from Lexington to Paris. The skeleton of the original Lexington & Maysville company remained, and in 1869 Bourbon County voted to subscribe to $200,000 in its stock to complete the line from Paris to Maysville.[15]

More drawn out but equally as frustrating were the relations of certain central Kentucky counties to the Lexington & Big Sandy Railroad (later known as the Elizabethtown, Lexington & Big Sandy Railroad Company). Designed to tie the Bluegrass and environs to the rich mineral deposits of eastern Kentucky, the Big Sandy Railroad received by 1853 nearly $1 million in subscriptions from Fayette, Clark, Montgomery, Bath, Carter, and Greenup counties, and the city of Lexington. But despite this financial support and continuous prognostications of eternal riches once the line was built, only the link from Lexington to Mount Sterling was completed before the company was sold in foreclosure shortly before the Civil War.[16]

After several false starts, much languishing, and at least one reorganization, the Big Sandy began soliciting county courts anew for another round of stock subscriptions in 1869. After much agitation and some initial rejection, voters in Fayette, Clark, and Montgomery counties approved new subscriptions, but those in the poorer eastern counties of Bath, Carter, and Rowan rejected such propositions. The optimism in central Kentucky which underlay the new subscriptions quickly dissipated when in 1873, as skeptics predicted, the Big Sandy was sold to a group of New York speculators led by Collis P. Huntington, president of the Chesapeake & Ohio. In the next six years, the three county subscribers sued to enjoin the sale and elected a rival slate of company directors pursuant to a special statute requiring that a majority of the company's directors be Kentucky residents and that only paid-up shareholders could vote (the New York speculators had allegedly paid in only 1 percent of their sale price). Seeking to counteract the counties, the New York group sought unsuccessfully to buy up large blocs of county taxpayer tax certificates which entitled them to shares of stock. The stalemate was not resolved until 1879 when Huntington persuaded the counties to drop their litigation in return for his pledge to complete the road to Huntington, West Virginia, within three years. Although the road was finished in the autumn of 1881, it had failed to return any money to the county investors as of July 1890.[17]

The lure of eastern Kentucky also attracted Franklin, Scott, and Bourbon county promoters who sought local government investments in the Frankfort, Paris & Big Sandy Railroad, which would compete with the Elizabethtown, Lexington & Big Sandy and other proposed east-west ventures. Such requests produced sharp controversy in Bourbon County. Soon after obtaining their charter, organizers of the railroad petitioned the Bourbon County Court to place on the August 1871 ballot a $300,000 stock subscription proposal. Seizing upon the fact that the charter allowed county courts the power to reject as well as accept railroad petitions, Bourbon County Court judge Richard Hawes refused to submit the proposition to the voters on the grounds that the proposed route would duplicate those already in existence or soon to be in existence.[18]

Undaunted by Hawes's refusal, friends of the railroad organized a committee to rally support. On August 23 Scott countians voted to subscribe, and a week later the *Paris True Kentuckian* added fuel to the drive by endorsing the subscription. Buoyed by this fresh support, the railroad petitioned the county court anew in December, increasing the proposed subscription to $400,000. Hawes led opposition to the proposition before the court of claims, this time citing the influx of black voters in addition to needless duplication of railroad lines. Blacks, who owned little property and paid few taxes, would support the proposition to secure work, he argued. Apparently agreeing with Hawes, the Bourbon court voted against submitting the question to voters.[19]

Having exhausted its remedies before the county court, officials of the railroad turned next to the legislature, petitioning it to alter the company's charter to require the Bourbon justices to place the subscription on the ballot. This latest ploy sparked a heated debate between proponents of the railroad and county court over the merits of the road and the proper place of the tribunal within the state constitution. Defenders of the court denounced the railroad's attempt to thwart the decision of the duly constituted authority of Bourbon County. Supporters of the railroad in turn castigated the court for denying the right of the voters to decide the subscription question for themselves. The people could not always be trusted to know what was best, countered court supporters, and besides, it was increasingly questionable whether a majority should ever be allowed to impose railroad taxation on a minority. Still others denied that the freedmen would overwhelmingly support the railroad and suggested the opposite might be true, while detractors of the project forecast a floating black laboring force foisting stock subscriptions off on counties across the entire nation.[20]

In early April 1872 the General Assembly ended one phase of the argument by amending the company's charter to require that the court submit the question to voters on April 27. Debate now shifted essentially to the merits of the subscription. On the appointed day, voters endorsed the proposed subscription 1,672 to 1,384, and at its June term the county court voted to subscribe to the company's stock. But the failure of the railroad to obtain sufficient subscriptions from other sources prevented it from beginning construction, allowing the Bourbon County Court to cancel its subscription without ever having advanced a cent, and concluding a controversy that was far from settled by the close vote in April.[21]

Hardened by earlier financial disasters and faced with even greater numbers of proposed subscriptions, county voters tended to be more cautious concerning railroad ventures following the Civil War. County judges and justices of the peace too were more chary, sometimes demanding that railroads complete lines through their counties before issuing bonds and more frequently demanding that legislatures give them the right to refuse to submit propositions to voters and then exercising that right. County officials such as Judge Logan Cockerell of Estill County personally took to the stump on occasion to oppose railroad subscriptions. Certain groups of citizens sometimes refused to abide by votes endorsing subscriptions. A mob in Washington County, for example, attacked a construction crew of the Cumberland & Ohio Railroad Company, burning tools and wagons, even though the voters had endorsed a subscription to the road by a margin of four to one. By 1881 many agreed with the *Mt. Sterling Sentinel*'s declaration that taxpayers would no longer tolerate public financing of private transportation schemes.[22]

Opponents of public investment in railroads found many allies in their quest to repudiate bond issues which resulted from fraud and which financed failures. Naturally most county courts sought to avoid liability on bonds issued to pay for railroads which were never started or if started, never completed. Bondholders just as often contested repudiation in state and federal courts, and in almost every case judges held that the counties remained liable for their debts even though they were products of misrepresentation and failure of consideration. Some disputes reached the United States Supreme Court which likewise upheld the liability of counties. Despite these judicial pronouncements, county resistance to payment continued; county courts, responding to writs of mandamus, levied special taxes to pay judgments on defaulted bonds and appointed tax collectors. Tax collectors either refused to accept the job or could not collect taxes from angry taxpayers, whereupon chagrined bondholders petitioned federal or state courts to appoint special tax collectors; but the Supreme Court ruled that such relief was beyond the powers of the judiciary. Possessed with judgments that were unenforceable, bondholders either lost their investments entirely or were forced to accept compromise settlements authorized by special legislation.

Muhlenberg County's railroad experience illustrates many of the frustrations of bonded indebtedness. In 1868 the county subscribed to $400,000 of the stock of the Elizabethtown & Paducah Railroad Company and issued bonds in that amount to pay for the stock. In the midst of the depression of 1873 the railroad went bankrupt, and in the process of reorganization the county's stock interest was wiped out. Since the railroad had never actually delivered the stock certificates to the county and since only part of the track had been laid, residents of Muhlenberg County believed that they had been the victims of a swindle. In 1874 outraged citizens organized the Independent Order of Taxpayers and elected a county judge committed to repudiation. In the same year the county court stopped paying interest on the bonds, thereby setting off a twenty-five-year fight between the county and bondholders.[23]

In March 1878 the Muhlenberg County Court secured special legislation from the General Assembly authorizing the election of a funding board empowered to compromise the railroad debt. The board met almost monthly between June 1878 and December 1880, but accomplished little in the way of compromise. What few bonds it did issue in settlement of outstanding indebtedness were themselves repudiated. By August 1882 the board had fallen into such disrepute that the voters refused to participate in the election of new members, and the county court had to appoint replacements. Confronted with an ineffective funding board and a defiant county court, bondholders commenced suing in state and federal circuit courts to compel payment on the bonds. Between 1888 and 1896 aggrieved bondholders obtained at least $159,000 in judgments against the county, which was ordered by the courts to levy and collect taxes at a rate amounting to at least $11.55 per $100 of valuation. The county complied with court orders, levying special taxes to satisfy judgments and appointing tax collectors. But tax collectors refused to qualify or failed to collect, and the courts refused to appoint their own collectors on the grounds that tax collecting was exclusively a local function. One bondholder would not be stymied by the judicial impasse and hired a private army to enforce his judgment, but other plaintiffs went unsatisfied. Taxpayers succeeded in evading most special taxes, but suffered a deepening recession as settlers, entrepreneurs, and potential consumers avoided a county whose indebtedness by 1890 encompassed half of the assessed valuation of its property. Finally in 1898 Muhlenberg countians elected a county judge committed to settlement of the debt. Shortly thereafter, he secured a compromise of the outstanding bonds at twenty cents on the dollar, payable over a twenty-year period. By 1906 the county was paying off its new bonds in a timely fashion and residents were enjoying newfound prosperity.[24]

Other counties suffered through experiences similar to Muhlenberg's. The defunct Cumberland & Ohio Railroad brought grief to several counties, including Marion. In 1873 residents organized into vigilante groups and forced the sheriff-elect to promise not to collect the railroad tax, a pledge that went unfulfilled as the county court somehow managed to collect taxes to pay off the railroad over the next twenty years. Green countians resisted more fiercely and effectively. Irate taxpayers plunged the county into "a frightful state of disorder and anarchy," burning down the barn of the railroad tax collector and threatening to do the same to the house of his surety if he did not stop collecting taxes. Neighboring Taylor County, refusing to be taxed for payment of its railroad debt, offered its worthless stock in settlement of its obligations. Allen County justices escaped imprisonment for contempt of court when the Supreme Court ruled that the judiciary had no authority to appoint a receiver of county taxes which no countian would collect. Although some suggested that the state assume the counties' indebtedness, the General Assembly rejected such attempts. Most counties had compromised their indebtedness by 1900, although a few entered the twentieth century persisting in their devotion to repudiation.[25]

A safe investment did not immunize counties from disputes with railroad companies over shareholder rights, taxation, and rights of way. Shareholder conflicts often involved complexities such as whether Hardin County was entitled to stock dividends in an amount equal to interest due on the county's total investment in the Louisville & Nashville Railroad Company or whether the Mobile & Ohio Railroad Company could sell an additional $500,000 without permission from its shareholders including McCracken County. In contrast, county court suits against railroad companies for damage to highways usually presented rather simple questions: for example, in 1889 Greenup County secured a decree in equity compelling the Maysville & Big Sandy Railroad to restore a public highway to its former condition, its having been altered by the company's construction crew. Other taxation disputes concerning livelier questions sometimes excited citizens as well as county officials. Particularly galling to many was the Court of Appeals ruling in 1868, settling a question which had been seething for over a decade, that railroads were liable for only state and not county taxation. Public outrage over this decision, and the deteriorating condition of its investments in railroads generally, prompted the General Assembly to overrule this decision implicitly by statute in 1876, a fact confirmed by the Court of Appeals eleven years later. Such legislation did not deter railroads from continuing to resist county taxation wherever possible and from seeking statutory exemption from the taxation of particular counties.[26]

Amid the clamor for the railroad, internal improvement supporters did not reduce their enthusiasm for sophisticated systems of turnpikes. At the very least, macadamized roads were necessary to convert individual counties into commercial integrals and to keep them competitive with their neighbors. "The old system of dirt roads [was] one of the most expensive and most worthless nuisances extant." A few zealots even claimed that collective county wealth would as much as quadruple if county courts adopted ambitious turnpike programs. As a result, investments in turnpike companies did not diminish during the period of the third constitution, although new sources of funds developed. As in the case of capital for railroad construction, the counties furnished a major portion of funds for turnpikes.[27]

A general recognition of the need for good county roads did not signify automatic approval of turnpike taxes. For even in the most prosperous counties, voters and county courts sometimes opposed propositions proclaimed as indispensable. Despite long-standing support from the *Cynthiana News*, in one case the voters of Harrison County resisted an ambitious program of tax support for turnpikes until November 1868 and supported it then by only a narrow margin. Many counties simply could not afford good roads, and often their geography made the construction of even simple paths difficult. As late as 1886 the *Frankfort Daily Capital* estimated that only half of Kentucky's 119 counties had any turnpikes or gravel roads and that thirty of these had fewer than twenty-five miles of such roads.[28]

Perhaps Harrison County's difficulties in enlisting voter support of turnpike projects, as well as those of other local governments, prompted the legislature in 1869 to enact a statute permitting county courts to subscribe as much as $1,000 per mile for the stock of turnpike companies without voter approval. But even a liberal use of this provision did not prove wholly satisfactory. In Franklin County, for example, although the court of claims promised to contribute to the building of nearly eighteen miles of new roads per year, the *Frankfort Commonwealth* argued that this would be insufficient to keep Franklin competitive with surrounding counties. Only a very detailed defense of the county's road plan pointing out the already heavy tax burden and the necessity for careful rather than hasty engineering quelled the journalistic complaints.[29]

More chagrined were the inhabitants of Benson Valley in the same central Kentucky county, whose existing road was washed out most of the year and who had long complained about the discriminatory county turnpike policy which had left them as the lone district without a macadamized route to Frankfort. The 1869 statute was of no benefit to them as the county court shortly thereafter determined not to contribute to turnpike projects not managed by private companies. Valley citizens brought on most of their problems themselves, long delaying the organization of a private company and then refusing to fund it adequately so that it might be eligible for county investment.

When at last the company obtained sufficient capital, it began squabbling with the county court over the proper route of the proposed turnpike. Even as work began in 1879 on the Pea Ridge route, dissidents in the valley submitted that the Buzzard Roost route was preferable.[30]

Although counties frequently made the largest investments in turnpike companies, management of these concerns remained largely out of their hands. Whatever leverage county courts had as principal stockholders was sometimes lost when companies, often poorly operated, were sold in satisfaction of mortgages. Reformers called for county courts to exercise more control over turnpike companies, but most turnpike legislation simply addressed itself to the protection of county investments. By the end of Reconstruction, many travelers complained that turnpike companies specialized in high tolls and poor service. Regulation was needed, they claimed, to force companies to repair roads and lower tolls. When county courts and taxpayer groups did become agitated about turnpike companies, it was usually over liabilities for stock subscriptions and taxation, not about the quality of management. Occasionally the legislature would transfer all or part of the operation of companies over to county courts, but this was ordinarily done because roads had not been completed or because the companies had become insolvent, and seldom, if ever, because they failed to maintain their systems or because they charged excessive rates.[31]

The absence of effective public control over privately operated turnpikes, for many the most important form of transportation available, produced increasingly loud cries for county courts to purchase the road companies and operate the systems toll-free. One of the earliest and, after a prolonged struggle, most successful movements for free turnpikes began in Fayette County following the Civil War. In October 1867 the *Kentucky Gazette* editorialized that the county court could purchase outstanding turnpike stock for twenty cents on the dollar and thereby eliminate the "female dragon" tollkeepers and the "deadhead" freeloaders who passed through the tollgates free of charge. Four years later, the *Gazette*'s recommendation seemed to gain wider recognition when the legislature authorized the state to sell its large turnpike holdings to the counties and several papers advocated statewide conversion to free turnpikes. Despite complaints, especially from Fayette County, that high tolls rendered urban centers into medieval cities walled off from the rural population and impeded travel in general, the free turnpike movement languished. The legislature repealed its statute authorizing sale of its turnpike stock and for a time county critics muffled their complaints.[32]

Fayette countians renewed their demands for toll-free roads in 1878 and persisted until voters approved conversion in 1890. While admitting Fayette's roads were generally "magnificent," a correspondent to the *Lexington Weekly Press* submitted that because of excessive tolls, farmers could afford to come to Lexington only on Saturdays and court day, and the newspaper itself agreed, labeling the Commonwealth's towns "quarantined areas." Dr. R. J. O'Mahoney, after intensive study, persuaded the Lexington Chamber of Commerce to advocate conversion and it, in turn, convinced the Fayette County Court to determine the feasibility of such a plan. Although critics of free turnpikes denounced the plan as impractical, too costly, and a violation of President Grover Cleveland's antipaternalism, proponents finally secured legislative permission to vote on the plan in August 1890. Fayette countians endorsed free turnpikes overwhelmingly, and the capital of the Bluegrass became one of the first to abolish tollroads. As the period of the modern constitution burgeoned in the 1890s, surrounding counties, including Scott, Bourbon, and Harrison, debated the question.[33]

In most counties variations of the original road law of Kentucky, inherited from colonial Virginia and England, prevailed throughout the period of the third constitution. Basically it provided that the county courts should divide the counties into districts and appoint a surveyor for each, with powers to compel all male residents between the ages of sixteen and fifty to work as many days as necessary to maintain the roads of the district. The statute specifically exempted ministers of the gospel from service and the courts could excuse the infirm. Although the legislature sometimes attempted sweeping reforms and often changed the laws of individual counties, the old system remained so much intact by 1890 that a delegate to the constitutional convention of that year could proclaim that Kentucky was one of only two or three states still retaining the forced labor system of road maintenance.[34]

Few openly defended the forced labor system. One who did was L. W. Lassing, delegate to the convention of 1890, who found the practice of forcing people to work on the roads an excellent way to extract contributions to government from people who otherwise would make none. Even poor people, he argued, used roads and should pay in some way for this usage. If Lassing was not bothered by the fact that in most counties (all after 1880) wealthier citizens could escape road work by paying a certain sum, others were, especially since the wealthy often owned lands whose value was enhanced by the work of the poor. Some went so far as to brand the practice as a "species of monarchial oppression" and a "most odious and unequal poll tax," while others saw it as a "sort of slavery in a land that boasts of its liberty." Most people simply regarded the system as "an utter failure."[35]

Critics described the typical road surveyor as dedicated above all to the evasion of his official duties. Although they allegedly possessed more power over their road hands than the governor, few bothered to do more work on their roads than it took to avoid grand jury indictment. Correspondents to newspapers often reported their travels over county roads filled with holes or almost completely washed out and often connected by unsafe bridges. The Court of Appeals once took notice that the "overseer of Gill Road [in Gallatin County] had failed for several years to have the same kept in good repair." But surveyors were not the only deficiencies in the system. Road hands were increasingly scarce either because they were exempted or because they fled to avoid service of work notices from the local road surveyor. And grand juries seldom indicted delinquent surveyors.[36]

The movement to reform the road law which began in the antebellum period gained momentum as the nineteenth-century matured, but never fully succeeded. As before, certain counties in the period of the third constitution gained legislative permission to poll their citizens on the question of adopting new systems, but these were often defeated; and the systems that were adopted were often incomplete. Some reform plans simply reduced the number of days of forced labor and provided for a payment of a tax in lieu of service. Others were more elaborate, calling for the appointment of a salaried road commissioner who would hire workers from funds provided by a special road tax ad valorem or poll or both. A correspondent from Union County in 1890 boasted that his county's reformed road law had produced an excellent system of roads for over twenty years even though none of them was macadamized. But such programs were not widespread; and while complaints about poor road maintenance reached a crescendo by the constitutional convention of 1890, that assembly decisively defeated two attempts to abolish the forced labor system.[37]

Counties had difficulty maintaining their buildings as well as their roads. The county judge and the justices of the peace as members of the court of claims were custodians of the county buildings, the most important of which were the courthouse and the jail. As such, they were charged with maintenance of these structures and the general upkeep of the public square, although the specific responsibility for day-to-day duties usually fell to the jailer and his deputies. The dilapidated condition of many of the county courthouses and jails of Kentucky created pressures upon the county governors to upgrade them by extensive repairs or entirely new construction. Their occasional refusals to do so sometimes nearly led them to incarceration in the very jails for which they were responsible.

Especially troublesome to the county courts were those jails. While critics often cited the deplorable conditions of many county jails, labeling them unsanitary and overcrowded, judges and justices were frequently reluctant to increase taxes to build new structures, or even to repair existing buildings. For their recalcitrance they were sometimes indicted by grand juries and even threatened with imprisonment for contempt of court. Yet, as in the case of Franklin County magistrates who were indicted nearly in every year between 1875 and 1886 for failing to build a new jail, almost no good was accomplished by these extreme measures. A postwar movement in some counties to supplement jails with workhouses as more satisfactory abodes in which to rehabilitate criminals only complicated the financial pressures upon the county governors.[38]

Observers often charged that courthouses were little better than the jails. The newspapers of Lexington variously described the Fayette County courthouse as the "Black Hole of Calcutta," "that hideous monster," "a miserable structure," and "a nuisance and a disgrace to the city and the county." The editor of the *Kentucky Gazette* went so far as to engage in an argument with the county judge about whether the steeple and weathercock of the ancient building were crooked. This agitation finally paid off in 1882 when the Fayette countians voted to build a new courthouse, which was completed in 1885. Occasionally criticism of county court custodianship extended to its supervision of the entire public square, as in Laurel County where the newspaper alleged that the conditions therein had "much to do with the spread of fever in the county seat." Similar problems occurred in many other counties, including Barren, Daviess, Whitley, Leslie, Trimble, Fulton, and Jackson.[39]

For all their unprofitability and periodic failures, county turnpike and railroad investments did produce some macadamized roads and railroad lines. The one major county-oriented river improvement project produced nothing but litigation and insolvency. Chartered shortly after the Civil War, the Kentucky

River Navigation Company mostly sought funds from counties bordering on the river of its name, the most important waterway of north-central Kentucky. The improvement of the river would supposedly assist in the exploitation of central Kentucky's great wealth, including large supplies of lead ore. Despite the optimism and puffing of its founders, the company obtained fewer county stock subscriptions than anticipated and suffered a crippling blow when the Court of Appeals ruled in the summer of 1871 that purported subscriptions of the Mercer and Garrard county courts in the amount of $175,000 had only been nonbinding proposals to subscribe. Thereafter other county courts refused to turn over taxes collected to pay for binding stock subscriptions and the company soon went into insolvency. While county courts worried about what to do with the unexpended taxes, creditors of the company unsuccessfully attempted to attach them.[40]

Frustrations produced by massive county railroad indebtedness helped push the Commonwealth to constitutional revision in 1890-1891. The revisers considered county debt limitation a principal object of their endeavors. After considerable debate, the delegates approved a series of restrictions on the ability of counties and cities to borrow money for internal improvements. Counties could not impose taxes at a rate exceeding fifty cents on the hundred dollars unless "it should be necessary . . . for the extinction of indebtedness contracted before the adoption of this Constitution." No county could become indebted "to an amount exceeding in any year the income and revenue provided for such year without the assent of two-thirds of the voters thereof." No county could incur indebtedness in excess of 2 percent of the amount of its assessed taxable property unless to liquidate an existing debt. With these provisions the framers of Kentucky's fourth constitution hoped to avoid a recurrence of the internal improvements binge which plunged many of their local governments into conditions of virtual bankruptcy during the period of the third constitution.[41]

8.
FISCAL CHAOS

Along with most Americans, nineteenth-century Kentuckians paid the bulk of their taxes to state and local governments. The county was the principal agent of assessment and collection while locally the court of claims set the county levy. The county assessor established property valuations for ad valorem taxes, both county and state. Primarily the sheriff collected taxes, although special collectors were sometimes appointed. Yet what was on paper a logical system was often in practice chaotic.

Although the framers of the third constitution provided for two associate judges to assist the county judge in fiscal matters, the legislature of 1850-1851 exercised the option of abolishing the associates and affiliating the justices of the peace with the county judge to form the court of claims. Its statutory duties were to lay the county levy, make all appropriations individually of $50 or over or collectively of $100 or over, transact the "other financial business of the county," and "erect and . . . keep a sufficient county jail." This system of county appropriations also left much to be desired.[1]

As with modern practice, the nineteenth-century tax assessment was essentially a self-regulated process. The county assessor distributed tax lists to taxpayers, who filled them out and returned them to the assessor after swearing to their accuracy. A county board of supervisors at first consisting of the county judge and county court clerk and eventually of one discrete taxpayer from each voting precinct, appointed by the county court, annually audited the assessor's tax book, noting delinquencies and correcting misvaluations. Valuations were used as the basis of assessing state taxes, which were entirely ad valorem on realty and selected personalty, and of special county taxes increasingly used to supplement the traditional poll tax. The assessor also distributed and received lists of tithables for the poll tax.[2]

The basic county tax continued to be the poll tax. At the beginning of the period its maximum was $1.50 per tithe, but this amount was eventually raised to $3.00, although the legislature not infrequently authorized some counties to exceed these limits. In other cases, counties authorized to impose ad valorem taxation had to contend with a lower maximum. Before emancipation all white male persons over the age of twenty-one and all slaves over the age of sixteen were liable for the tax, while after the Civil War the liability simply rested on all male persons over the age of twenty-one. Courts of claims were permitted to issue excuses from liability to persons "on account of age, infirmity, or other charitable reasons."[3]

Politicians continued to debate the merits of the poll tax, its critics labeling it "oppressive" and a "relic of . . . a barbarous age." They argued that the tax was hardest on common laborers who were usually paid no more than fifty cents a day. A former county judge noted that he had "had the poor of my county coming to me . . . time and time again, and begging me to spare them the humiliation and degradation of being returned delinquent, regarding it second only to the brand of infamy placed upon the felon for some crime." Others cited Richard T. Ely's observation that "poll-taxes are unworthy of a civilized nation in the nineteenth century" and pointed out that most northern states had abolished them. Those few who publicly defended the exaction argued that the tax was necessary to fund poor relief which enabled those who could not afford the tax to receive much more because of it. As in the case of the road tax, the poll tax forced the propertyless to contribute something to their government.[4]

Some of the poor may have complained about the tax, but

most apparently did not pay it; delinquency rates in many counties were high. In Pulaski County, for example, observers estimated that of 5,100 tithables, 1,100 were annually returned as delinquent, while in Washington County a local official reported that of approximately 3,500 tithables, 700 were delinquent. Many tithables secured relief under a provision which permitted the court of claims to excuse the aged and infirm. In one unidentified "mountain county," a courtroom visitor reported that "the entire time of the court during the first day of its session was taken up in relieving persons from the poll-tax," while in Laurel County the local newspaper lambasted the court of claims for exempting all old men regardless of wealth. But despite the constant objections, efforts to abolish the tax both during the period of the third constitution and the constitutional convention of 1890-1891 failed.[5]

As expenses such as railroad and turnpike subscriptions and building repair and construction became more ordinary, legislatively authorized county ad valorem taxation became fairly commonplace. While the legislature limited most county ad valorem taxation to a period of years, it did permit some that were open-ended, such as that for Bracken County, which authorized the county court to levy its tax "from year to year until the whole debt due by the county is fully liquidated." Nor did the legislature always establish a maximum tax rate. Legislation was passed in 1868 allowing county courts to levy an ad valorem tax "as may be required" to pay claims, indebtedness, and complete or repair public buildings.[6]

Opposition to county enforcement of local and state taxation ranged from the chronic complaints which invariably accompany taxation to profound outrage from officials and taxpayers alike over gross inequities, inconsistencies, and inadequacies. Tax increases were almost certain to produce some outcry. The situation in Fulton County in southwestern Kentucky was typical. Critics charged in 1877 that the county court had doubled the poll tax from $1.50 to $3.00 in order to build a bridge for an isolated part of the county with only six inhabitants; the court of claims denied wrongdoing, asserting that the high rate was due solely to an underestimation of delinquencies. Similarly, a Whitley County resident demanded a full accounting of his county's finances after his county court had doubled the poll tax in the spring of 1876, and Robertson County citizens petitioned the General Assembly for a refund of all county levies paid for the year 1867. Similar complaints emerged from Harrison and Laurel counties, where people decried steadily increasing taxation with no relief from indebtedness. In the latter community, taxation became a partisan issue with Republicans accusing Democrats of raising taxes by almost 100 percent during their four-year administration, and the Republican candidate for county judge promising to resign if he failed to lower taxes in the event he won office.[7]

Complaints about deficiencies in tax assessment and collection were more justified. For years the legislature and state officials groped for a solution to what amounted to widespread tax evasion by substantial numbers of would-be taxpayers. The representation that "many persons in this Commonwealth have for several years failed to list their property either with the assessor for their counties or with the county court" prompted the General Assembly in 1862 to require that the state auditor appoint sixteen revenue agents to look into the problem of tax collection in general. While this legislation apparently helped remedy the problem of tax collection, the attendant problems of evasion and underevaluation did not abate. In 1873 Governor P. H. Leslie complained that thousands of taxpayers concealed taxable property while assessors practiced gross inconsistencies in their evaluations. A decade later, Governor J. Proctor Knott reported that while sheriffs were collecting taxes with unprecedented success, assessments remained inconsistent and undervalued. Knott asserted that urban property was never assessed more than 60 percent of true value, while rural property seldom reached 40 percent. Inconsistencies in evaluations prevailed between classes of taxpayers and localities with wealthier citizens and regions the most seriously underassessed. With derision, the governor noted that Boyd County horses were assessed at a greater value than those in Bourbon County, although the latter were of much higher quality. Knott's complaints prompted the legislature to establish a state board of equalization, which in turn produced more equality but not higher assessments. Two years later, Governor Knott alleged that even though Indiana had fewer acres of taxable realty, its assessed value was twice that of Kentucky's.[8]

County officials so defectively executed the tax laws that in the late 1870s taxpayer revolts broke out in many counties, including Kenton, Campbell, Bracken, Owen, Grant, Harrison, and Pendleton, and in the Commonwealth generally taxpayer unrest was reported to be widespread. Of these the Pendleton County affair is most completely documented and revealing.[9]

Pendleton County's taxpayer revolt was embodied in a committee of safety appointed by a mass meeting of citizens in early 1877. Shortly after its creation and pursuant to instructions from the "mass of citizens," the committee laid before the Pendleton court of claims "some of the grievances of which our people complain." Submitting that there were four sets of tax collectors "at work in our midst," the committee charged that heavy taxation was burdening "the productive portion of our population" and "retarding the development of the resources of our county." In some cases, the committee further noted, in order to satisfy delinquencies the tax-gatherers had taken from poor families their last horse or cow "or the very bed upon which they sleep." Arguing that the "distress" was so common that it was undoubtedly well known to the magistrates, the committee explained that Pendletonians had heretofore borne the hardship in the belief that it was necessary to liquidate a large county debt. The absence of visible public improvements and the failure of the county court to issue annual financial statements prompted them to abandon their patient stance and issue a series of demands.[10]

The committee requested that the court suspend the extraordinary levy made at the November 1876 term of a four-dollar poll tax and a relatively high ad valorem tax until the magistrates had audited and published the county's financial accounts. It urged the justices to obtain delinquent taxes and other receivables from the county officers and ex-officers who should have collected them and to shorten the period in which such officials had to settle their accounts. It asserted that ex-sheriffs and other tax collectors were given too much time in which to complete their unfinished business and that the latter should be turned over to their successors. Finally, it submitted that much property in the county was unassessed and demanded that it be assessed.[11]

Although tabling the committee's address, the county court of claims did respond to it in part by appointing a special committee to study the problem of delinquent taxes. When the special committee reported that over $25,000 was owed the county in delinquent taxes over a fourteen-year period, the court of claims elected James T. Clark back tax collector. Meanwhile the *Falmouth Independent* advocated the appointment of a county auditor "to keep the finances of the county in an intelligent and correct shape," and the committee of safety urged those taxpayers listed as delinquent, but who in fact had paid their taxes, to seek assistance from the committee and accused the sheriffalty of a faulty tax receipt system. The committee also charged its county tax officialdom of conspiring to wrest valuable land from innocent owners by forced tax sales after deliberately failing to collect taxes.[12]

In March 1877 the Pendleton County grand jury commenced investigating allegations of corrupt and incompetent county tax policies and practices. Its decision to issue no indictments and pass the inquiry back to the county court produced an accusation from the *Covington County Ticket* that the criminal court judge and commonwealth's attorney had packed the jury with ex-county officers and their relatives, a charge denied by the *Falmouth Independent*. The committee of safety was apparently content with the jury's inaction as it recommended that any prosecution of county officers for fraudulent tax practices be postponed until the county court had looked into the matter. But the committee did not relax its vigilance as it accused the incumbent sheriff of owing $16,000 in delinquent taxes and resolved to expose the absurdities of a hastily issued county court financial statement. Perhaps cowed by the environment of suspicion and investigation, ex-sheriff B. B. Mullins issued a claim that he had collected and accounted for all delinquent taxes during his term of office, but that the county court clerk had failed to record the transactions and the back tax collector was attempting to collect taxes from those who had already paid them.[13]

The committee of safety further expanded its lists of grievances and proposed reforms at another mass meeting of citizens held on court day in May 1877. It branded the county court's financial statement as inaccurate and accused officials of collecting taxes but not recording the payments, of borrowing money for public purposes and then appropriating it for their own use, of failing to account for taxes collected on unassessed property, and of neglecting to assess the property of nonresidents. The committee urged the abolition of these evils and the elimination of consecutive terms for sheriffs. Undaunted by the aura of crisis and scandal, the Pendleton County Court refused to consider the committee of safety's exposé of the county financial statement on the grounds that the committee's members had not signed it and adjourned without considering the grand jury's request for an investigation of county finances. But it did go on record in opposition to legislative extensions of time for sheriffs to collect taxes and in support of tougher laws against speculation in county claims.[14]

Charges and countercharges, denials and rebuttals continued to dominate county governmental news throughout the remainder of 1877. County court clerk Jonathan B. Applegate admitted that he had not kept a record of tax collections, but argued that he had no legal responsibility to do so, an assertion denied by J. W. Woodhead, chairman of the committee of safety. Several correspondents to the *Falmouth Independent* accused

James T. Clark, collector of back taxes, of attempting to collect from those who had already paid and, in addition, of favoritism and inconsistency in the execution of his official responsibilities. Clark vehemently denied these charges. Finally the grand jury, spurred on by the continuous blasts of the committee of safety and the biting editorials of the *Independent*, censured county officials for negligent tax collecting and reporting, and indicted the court of claims for failing to publish a statement of the debts and assets of the county.[15]

As the 1878 campaign for county offices approached, the committee of safety sought to broaden its crusade into general governmental reform. Its chairman, J. W. Woodhead, proclaimed that the committee would work through local "county reform clubs" of from fifty to a hundred members each to rid local government of the professional officeholders, office seekers, and "their hangers-on" who constituted nearly half of the adult population of the county. Officials must make government more responsive to the needs of the people, Woodhead declared, and his committee would seek to keep partisan politics out of county government. Several neighborhoods organized reform clubs, and a mass meeting at the Lick Creek Precinct defended Woodhead against unspecified charges of immorality. At year's end the committee sponsored still another mass county meeting and there called for more efficient collection and disbursement of revenues and pledged that its people would not support any candidate for county office, regardless of his party affiliation, if he had "heretofore proved himself either unwilling or incompetent to perform his duties."[16]

The new year saw the committee of safety intensify its political activities. It issued specific interrogatories for James T. Clark, collector of back taxes, and when his answers were judged unresponsive, it appointed a special committee to pursue the questioning further. It promulgated more general queries for all candidates for county office, seeking their views on tax reform and fiscal responsibility. It requested that the county's legislative representatives publish all bills affecting the county so that the committee and citizens in general could comment upon them, and it sponsored public discussions of county governmental problems and policy.[17]

Despite the flurry of committee activity between early 1877 and mid-1879, it is doubtful that it had a lasting impact on the quality of Pendleton County government. The committee enjoyed more success in revelation than in reform. It demonstrated that past and present county tax officials had failed to account for taxes collected, to collect large amounts of taxes due, and to assess still other large amounts of taxable property. Despite renewed committee agitation and claims of jury-packing, grand juries called in 1878 and 1879 continued to avoid a thorough investigation into county court affairs, and previous indictments came to naught. Some tax reduction was secured, as well as a general commitment of the court of claims and county officials to keep and publish more complete records, but there is no evidence of marked improvement in assessment and collection practices. Significantly, one of the last reported actions of the committee was its plea to aggrieved taxpayers to initiate themselves individual civil suits and criminal charges, a confession that its call for governmental action had largely failed.[18]

Tax assessment and collection were only part of the fiscal problem for the counties and their governors. Taxpayers, journalists, and even county officials also criticized county appropriations and expenditures, as well as tax assessments and collections. Complainants cited both general and specific deficiencies in the fiscal planning of courts of claims. Most of the reported challenges concerned specific appropriations, and not a few originated from county officials themselves. In 1869 Fayette County's Judge Graves disputed the right of his court of claims to appropriate $1,500 for the Orphan Society of Lexington on the grounds that it was unconstitutional and illegal for a county to spend taxpayers' money for a private institution not under the control of the government. At first refusing to sign the minutes containing the expenditure, Judge Graves ultimately decided to challenge it before the courts. While the Fayette County Circuit Court ruled in his favor, the Court of Appeals sustained the court of claims on the grounds that the statutory provision requiring county courts to provide for the poor was broad enough to permit the appropriation. Twenty years later the Fayette County Court became embroiled in a similar dispute. Some on the court wished for it to appropriate $200 for the privately controlled Home of the Friendless, but justice of the peace Henry Payne and several others protested on the grounds that certain of the inmates were immoral. Payne's accusations provoked a fistfight between himself and "Squire Jewell," and a spirited defense of the home from certain female members of its board of directors. In the end, Justice Payne apologized and the court approved the expenditure.[19]

Most of the challenges to proposed county expenditures came from individual taxpayers. Although the Court of Appeals severely restricted the ability of private citizens to thwart court of claims' appropriations through litigation, ruling, for example, that an aggrieved taxpayer could not enjoin the Pendleton County Court from purchasing a site for a poor farm, it could not put a stop to continuous complaints from the general public. In an episode similar to Fayette County's, the *Cynthiana News* denounced the Harrison County Court in 1868 for appropriating county tax funds for Harrison Academy and assuming part of its debt even though the school was privately owned and operated and the county judge was one of the trustees. One of the academy's trustees, M. L. Broadwell, put to rest some public resentment over the expenditure, when he pointed out that a statute authorized the county court appropriation and that the academy had been a public school for the past two and one-half years. But three years later, a correspondent to the *News* delivered an unanswered blast against the Harrison County Court for giving poor relief to nonpaupers. In other examples, a Robertson County resident questioned the legality of an 1875 appropriation of his county's court of claims for a railing around the courthouse rostrum, while ten years later a member of the Franklin County Court denied reports that his tribunal had made an excessive appropriation to a superintendent of a local bridge project.[20]

If the ordinary citizen did not have standing to question court of claims financial policy in general, he clearly could dispute decisions which affected claims for services he had rendered the county, and such controversies were so frequent as to be routine. Although many of the disputes were never litigated, a number of those which were concerned claims of doctors who had performed services for the county. In a series of cases the Court of Appeals ruled that despite the existence of an emergency, doctors could not be reimbursed for services to the county unless they secured approval from the court of claims, and perhaps even the local board of health, and not simply the county judge.[21]

Bickering over appropriations and claims constituted an inevitable problem of government; trafficking in those claims represented a far more serious difficulty. Even after the so-called age of democratic reform, governments in nineteenth-century America still retained some of the personal qualities of their neo-medieval predecessors. While offices and perquisites were no longer formally bought, sold, and transferred like personalty to relatives and friends, informally such was often the case. This was especially true in the area of claims against the county government for goods sold and services performed. Although a state statute made it a crime for "any county judge, justice of the peace, sheriff, county clerk, or county attorney to traffic for, purchase, or speculate in any claim or claims, to be allowed by the court of claims of the county of which he or they may be said judge," this prohibition was not effectively enforced and did not apply either to other county officers or to the public at large.[22]

Claims brokers flourished in nineteenth-century Kentucky in part because of the awkwardness of claims processing and funding. County creditors had to wait until their services were performed before presenting their claims to the county court, which sat as a court of claims no more than twice a year and usually only once. After the court approved the claim, the creditor had to wait at least six months for the sheriff to collect enough taxes to pay off the county's debts. For those creditors without ample cash reserves or who were on the county payroll, the only recourse was to sell their claims to a broker at a substantial discount. The broker would eventually turn a handsome profit when the tax collector finally paid off. Although critics periodically denounced such institutional usury, little was done in the way of effective reform during the period of the third constitution. Statutes such as the one which required the Marshall County Court to hold two claims courts per year and to pay off all claims within two to four months of each term offered as their only penalty recourse against the tax collector. As late as 1885 the *Frankfort Capital* urged sheriffs to collect and pay their taxes expeditiously and fully so that schoolteachers would not have to "pass through the ruthless hands of 'claims brokers.' " Not only did sheriffs seldom heed such demands, but there is evidence that they and their deputies were among the most active of the brokers.[23]

Most legislative reform efforts centered not on the problem of slow claims liquidation but on the question of ascertaining the validity and size of claims and their amounts. Critics cited the "cumbersome" machinery of claims processing which led to "confusion . . . irregularity [and] conflicting opinions." Some courts either summarily accepted all claims and thereby sent tax rates soaring or arbitrarily halved all claims, which cheated honest creditors and rewarded the dishonest ones who, in anticipation of such practices, doubled or trebled the amount of their claims. Statutory reforms generally required claims to be presented to the county clerk's office at least ten days before the convening of claims courts so that the county attorney, who was charged with screening all claims, could adequately pass upon them before presenting them to the full court. Some counties were authorized to appoint special claims commissioners, but these experiments were usually short-lived. The legislature sometimes attempted to redress the hastiness of claims approval in some counties by permitting only half of the justices of the peace to act with the county judge as the court of claims, but this reform proved to be as ineffectual as the others.[24]

Reformers tried other ways to combat increasingly scandalous and chaotic county fiscal management. In 1860, after a stream of complaints about government by secrecy, the legislature enacted a statute requiring all county clerks to publish annually a statement of "the debts and assets of the county, the allowances by the court, to whom, and for what purpose made." Yet this statute was not uniformly observed, and when it was enforced, it often did nothing but reveal a county's "muddled" accounts. For this reason, some counties obtained legislative authority to appoint a county auditor whose task it was to keep a full account of all county funds, receipts, and disbursements, to insure that collections were received and expenditures properly expended, and, presumably, to bring some semblance of order out of confusion. But there is no evidence that the few counties which appointed auditors found them to be a panacea for their fiscal turmoil.[25]

Eleven counties, or fewer than one-tenth, adopted the most radical and successful reform of fiscal control: they abandoned their courts of claims entirely and secured legislative authorization to elect three-man boards of commissioners, who were empowered to perform all the duties of the traditional fiscal courts. Normally the commissioners were elected for three years, although in Magoffin County the circuit court judge appointed three commissioners annually. Oddly enough no one appears to have questioned the constitutionality of the commission system under the third constitution even though section 29 of that document offers some support for the notion that the General Assembly could choose between only two alternative fiscal courts: one consisting of "a presiding judge and two associate judges" or a presiding judge and "any or all of the justices of the peace" of the county. And certainly the Magoffin County plan of circuit court-appointed commissioners seems even more constitutionally suspect, although it, too, apparently was never challenged.[26]

Proponents of the commission system argued that it was more efficient and less expensive than the traditional court of claims. Senator Charles D. Foote, sponsor of the bill establishing the Kenton County Commission, contended that his plan would attract businessmen to county government, while the old system repelled them because they did not wish to assume the judicial responsibilities of justices of the peace. He submitted further that three skilled businessmen could accomplish more than greater numbers of justices of the peace for less pay. All in all the new commissioners would work more efficiently and effectively at a savings to the taxpayers. Others supported Foote's reasoning, submitting that many justices of the peace were ignorant of business procedures and that unless the county judge and county attorney were "intelligent and painstaking," claims courts often deteriorated into "very exasperating spectacles" for those there on business while providing "entertainment" for spectators. Though many praised the success of the new fiscal courts, delegates to the 1890-1891 constitutional convention refused to make them mandatory and simply codified the status quo by giving counties the option of adopting them.[27]

Counties were able to transfer some local expenses to the state. Traditionally the Commonwealth paid most of the costs of criminal law enforcement and the entire cost of maintaining pauper idiots and purchasing county record books. The state auditor accused many counties of passing off large numbers of their poor as idiots so that the state would underwrite their poorhouses. In an effort to curtail this abuse, the legislature in 1882 transferred the jurisdiction in cases of idiocy from county and police courts to circuit courts, but the remedy proved very temporary. In 1885 the auditor complained that circuit courts were no more vigilant than their predecessors in jurisdiction and that the numbers of alleged pauper idiots continued to multiply each year. Five years later the General Assembly partially confronted the problem by requiring the counties to pay twenty dollars of the annual maximum allowance per idiot of seventy-five dollars. State officials never did convince the legislature of the wisdom of requiring counties to pay for their own record books.[28]

The method of paying county officials constituted another neo-feudalistic characteristic of the local constitution. Fees and not salaries constituted the primary source of income for most county officials. Only the county judge and county court attorney received a formal salary, and each of them received additional income, the former from a limited number of fees and the latter from a percentage of all fines and forfeitures for successful misdemeanor prosecutions. The remaining officers depended entirely upon fees for their official income.[29]

The amount of fee income received by a county official depended directly on the amount of legal business transacted in his county. Officers of poorer, less sophisticated, and more sparsely populated counties naturally drew less money from fees than those of richer and more heavily populated counties. While county offices of pauper counties sometimes went abegging because of inadequate income, those of the wealthiest sometimes commanded immense incomes and attracted hordes of aspirants. In Jefferson County, the most heavily populated of the state, the jailer earned from $30,000 to $40,000 per year, while the sheriff and county clerk earned a minimum of $10,000. Naturally, these lucrative offices attracted highly organized and well-financed candidacies. Critics charged that incumbents created "corruption funds" from portions of their profits with which to wage reelection campaigns by vote-buying and other illegal methods. Yet an intensive investigation by a legislative committee in 1879-1880 turned up no illegal fee-charging by Jefferson County officers. However, an observer did uncover widespread fee-gouging elsewhere, especially in the pauper counties of the east, where sheriffs and other law enforcement officers reportedly conspired with others to create fraudulent arrests, enjailments, and even trials in order to collect fees from the Commonwealth.[30]

Not surprisingly, the fee system produced criticism and calls for its abolition. The *Louisville Evening Post*, a leading opponent of the system, branded it "a tax upon justice," which enabled county officers, especially those from wealthier counties, "to get better pay and do less work than any class of citizens in the commonwealth." If the system was not corrupt, it was at least oppressive. "Fees! Fees! Fees! Wherever you go there stands an officer, surrounded by henchmen and flatterers, who will work for him, vote for him, fight for him, and buy others to do the same," the *Post* lamented. But defenders of the system, reflecting an almost medieval perception of public office, maintained that an officer's fees were his personal property and that it was even beyond the power of a constitutional convention to take them away from him. The *Post* did, however, accurately observe that no reform group could topple the system during the period of the third constitution, this in part because of the great power of the fee collectors and their toadies.[31]

As with the odious fees, county salaries produced public uproar. The original statutes implementing the constitutional establishment of the office of county judge did not expressly provide for a salary, but most county courts had done so by the Civil War. While these early provisions for a guaranteed annual wage prompted some outcries, they paled in comparison to the protests which greeted salary increases after the war. The greatest turmoil occurred in the mid-1870s following the legislature's granting of misdemeanor jurisdiction to county judges, an expansion of responsibility which caused some courts of claims to increase the judges' salaries. Opponents lashed at such increases in Mason, Hickman, and Fayette counties, and despite resistance from those who charged that these attacks were motivated solely by narrow partisan political considerations, anti-increase forces in Fayette County succeeded in having increments rolled back. Fayette's struggle also involved allegations that the justices of the peace had for at least seven years overpaid themselves for their daily attendance at courts of claims. After they had been indicted for same by a grand jury, they reduced their own fees also. County judge salaries and those of the county attorney also sparked public debate in Grant, Harrison, Pendleton, and Lincoln counties, among others.[32]

County officers who might not be the objects of public derision were nearly always the victims of evasion and flight to avoid payment of fees. Apparently officials did not always collect fees upon performance of services, and fees receivable were sometimes difficult to collect. The statute books are full of special legislation extending the period in which county officers could lawfully collect their fee bills. Judges and court attorneys, especially those from pauper counties, occasionally had difficulty collecting their full salary allotments, and some even had to resort to litigation, but these grievances were more infrequent than those arising over fees.[33]

During the period of the third constitution, the counties continued to be the core of Kentucky's taxation system and as such were hardly models of efficiency and stability. Major problems of assessment and collection consistently plagued county officials and produced widespread popular unrest, in some places bordering on outright rebellion. Nor did the counties enjoy any more success as agencies of appropriation and expenditure. Cumbersome claims procedures placed large chunks of the counties' accounts payable in the hands of private brokers. The fee system also underlined the private, neo-feudalistic nature of county government and sometimes provoked public dismay and official corruption. Reformers attempted to cope with these problems, but not with much success, and their failure to centralize the state's fiscal operations served to highlight the parochial nature of the Commonwealth's constitution.

9.
CONCLUSION AND POSTSCRIPT

The Civil War settled the question of the ultimate sovereignty of the federal government, and the industrial and urban revolutions which followed it did much to draw Americans closer together in a physical, economic, and social sense. Yet during the remainder of the nineteenth century, the nation remained primarily rural in nature and local government continued to play a significant role in the lives of most citizens. This was especially true in Kentucky, where on the eve of constitutional reform in 1890 only 19.2 percent of the people lived in cities. If anything, county government came to affect Kentuckians even more intimately during the period of the third constitution. Counties invested the most governmental funds in internal improvements, built and maintained most of the roads, and continued to act as the primary enforcer of laws for most of the Commonwealth's residents. They also retained their responsibilities as the principal tax collectors and dispensers of poor relief. Competition for county offices in the newly inaugurated elective system constituted a significant phase of Kentucky's intense political life, and the official day on which the county courts met continued to be the foremost social and economic day of the month for most Kentuckians. At least in Kentucky, nineteenth-century state government largely confined itself to a few specialized services such as assistance to the physically and mentally handicapped, minimal regulation of a few industries and professions, aid to education, the operation of several small colleges, maintenance of a state guard, and operation of a judicial and penal system. Americans continued to look to local government for resolution of most of their public problems. The welfare state had not yet evolved. When the federal government attempted to intervene in state and local affairs for a brief period following the Civil War, it was the county governments which largely frustrated that endeavor.

Despite the good intentions of the reformers of 1849-1850, Kentucky's counties also maintained the tradition of parochialism, corruption, and inefficiency. Democracy cured few of the basic deficiencies of the local constitution. Fee-gouging persisted, vote-buying replaced office-auctioning, and the quality of public service remained low. Although the legislature created fewer new counties, its mounting preoccupation with local and special legislation rendered it almost a rubber stamp for the needs of counties and their citizens. Ostensibly an invasion of local autonomy, Kentucky's system of local legislation in reality constituted a crude form of county home rule. Besieged with requests for local statutes, legislators normally adhered to the desires of counties seeking special statutes and sometimes even allowed their officers to draft the legislation. In effect, the seekers of these special statutes became a third house of the legislature. Contrary to assumption, restrictions on local legislation in the fourth constitution represented limitations on county government, not a liberation of it.

Although theoretically a province of the state, counties constituted in many respects semi-autonomous entities. Their participation in the railroad binge encompassed a rivalry not unlike that between the city-states of fourteenth-century Italy. Without a chief executive officer, county officials themselves represented semi-autonomous constitutional creatures without direction either at home or from Frankfort. Despite the injection of democratic politics, the persistence of the fee system prompted most county officials to maintain a proprietary attitude toward their offices. In many ways, nineteenth-century Kentucky resembled medieval Europe.

CONCLUSION 143

A prevailing lawlessness compounded the semi-anarchical condition of many of Kentucky's counties. Crime, whether in the shape of feuds and vigilantism or in less organized forms, rendered the lives of many countians progressively insecure as the century matured. If county leaders failed to enforce the criminal law, they also often refused to honor their civil commitments, especially if they involved railroad indebtedness. Nineteenth-century Kentucky left no legacy of law and order.

The Constitution of 1891 largely retained Kentucky's county government. The new frame of government limited indebtedness, abolished the fee system in Jefferson County, and granted the legislature the option of abolishing the office of commonwealth's attorney and merging it into the county attorney's office, of merging the jailership with the sheriffalty, and abolishing the office of assessor. It also gave the legislature the right to abolish counties. Counties were given the option of adopting the commission form of government. The reformers changed little else.

In part because of the failure of the Constitution of 1891 to reform effectively, many of the nineteenth-century deficiencies of county government persisted into the twentieth. The fee system continued to debilitate the county officialdom, causing it to treat public office as a private concession. Writing in 1923 for the Efficiency Commission of Kentucky, H. S. Gilbertson, executive secretary of the National Short Ballot Organization and a pioneer in the study of county government, called for the abolition of the fee system, labeling it "unsound in principle, ineffective, and often grossly inequitable in practice." Kentucky's adherence to this antiquated system of compensation caused it to "occupy an exceedingly backward position in this respect among the states." Other students of the local constitution echoed this plea with no effect. Faced with vigorous opposition from scores of county officials, the legislature refused to take most county officials off the fee system and place them on salaries. Although the legislature did require fiscal courts to place limitations on the compensation of county officers, with surplus fees going to the fiscal courts, as recently as 1975 some officers reportedly continued to retain fees in violation of the statute.[1]

Some believed that justices of the peace remained mired in mediocrity and that the majority of county judges had deteriorated in quality by 1923. In the opinion of some, the majority of justices of the peace outside of eastern Kentucky had almost ceased to perform judicial functions except in Jefferson County, where they allegedly operated a network of speed traps. H. S. Gilbertson estimated that a majority of county judges lacked sufficient knowledge of the law to perform their judicial duties and that some rated as generally illiterate. Others argued that county judges often prevented greedy lawyers from converting the probate process into an assault on defenseless estates. In 1975, voters sided with critics of the system of local justice and approved a constitutional amendment stripping the justices of the peace and county judges of their judicial functions and transferring these duties to newly created district judges trained in the law.[2]

Some sheriffs continued to neglect the enforcement of criminal laws whether because of negligence or lack of funds (others performed remarkably well, although short of manpower and money). An appraisal of the Ohio County sheriff written in 1923 could easily have been written sixty years earlier: "the sheriff is not interested in serving warrants of any kind, either civil or criminal . . . [his] chief interest is in collecting taxes." The same commentator noted that similar conditions existed in other counties and that sheriffs especially refused to enforce prohibition laws. Making almost the identical summary in 1938, an observer reported that some counties attempted to bolster their inadequate systems of law enforcement by establishing county patrols but that these also proved ineffective. Advocating the abolition of the office of constable, the writer also proposed the establishment of a state police force. Ten years later, the legislature created a state police department, and following World War II, a number of urban counties founded

CONCLUSION   145

county police forces, a proposition sometimes advanced in the nineteenth century but seldom implemented. Most counties continued to depend on their sheriffs for law enforcement and not a few found the task increasingly difficult because of a shortage of funds. In 1975 the sheriff of Edmonson County donated the bulk of his personal fees to provide his county with twenty-four hour policing. Despite the sheriff's plight and his unselfish response to it, voters overwhelmingly rejected a special tax to provide better county law enforcement. Kentucky sheriffs argued that more compensation and the right to successive terms would enhance law enforcement, but the legislature and voters refused to approve these reforms.[3]

Gilbertson also downgraded most of the other county officers. County attorneys lacked courage and independence, some even breaching professional ethics. In one county, the school superintendent hired the county attorney to represent him in his settlement of accounts with the fiscal court and the Commonwealth so that the very same county attorney would not prosecute him for improper dispersal and accounting of funds. Another county attorney reportedly refused to prosecute local banks for charging the county excessive rates of interest because "he did not like to proceed against his neighbors." In 1923 the attorney general alleged that many county attorneys had no knowledge of even the fundamentals of law and could not perform the most rudimentary of their statutory duties. In the same year, Gilbertson for the Efficiency Commission echoed the plea of some at the constitutional convention of 1890-1891 that the office of commonwealth's attorney be merged into the office of county attorney in order to simplify prosecutorial duties and upgrade the latter office. He also proposed (to no avail) that seven assistant attorneys general be created to supervise the activities of the county attorneys.[4]

Jailers continued, because of negligence or because of antiquated jails, to suffer prison escapes, a condition reminiscent of the nineteenth century. In the early twentieth century some county clerks permitted records to be falsified, stolen, or destroyed by fire. One clerk left his office open at all hours of the day and night for the convenience of attorneys, a practice permitting one unscrupulous citizen to attempt unsuccessfully to alter a public document. The perversity of county politicians in regard to the county treasuryship knew no bounds. After the legislature finally recognized common practice and required county courts to elect the county treasurer on the basis of competitive bidding, the tribunals began to award the position to cronies or to the sheriff in defiance of the law and former custom.[5]

Although claims processing continued to be slipshod, with justices of the peace continuing to halve unfamiliar claims and unquestioningly approve those favored by a colleague, some progress occurred in the area of county budgeting. By a 1934 statute, the legislature required all counties to secure approval of their budgets by the state Department of Finance, which in practice required all counties to produce balanced budgets. Nonetheless, at least one commentator criticized the Commonwealth for imposing too much rigidity on county financial planning.[6]

Tax assessment and collecting continued to be a problem well into the new century. Although the state tightened its control over assessment and collection by virtue of the supervision of the State Tax Commission, the Auditor of Public Accounts, and the State Inspector and Examiner, and while the legislature replaced the office of county assessor with that of county tax commissioner, underassessment and nonassessment of taxable property persisted. John W. Manning, professor of political science at the University of Kentucky, attributed this to lack of good maps, cronyism, reliance on outdated evaluations, and uncooperative taxpayers. Manning also pronounced as a "farce" an examination administered by the Commonwealth to all prospective county tax commissioners. As of 1938 many sheriffs experienced difficulty in the collection of taxes, encountering the same problems as had their nineteenth-century counterparts.[7]

CONCLUSION 147

During the early period of the fourth constitution, some counties evaded restrictions on indebtedness, illegally incurring debts without securing voter approval. By 1936 most counties possessed indebtedness, and some repudiated their debts in the wake of depression. After World War II the state began exercising greater control over county debts and, in the opinion of one expert, steered the local units of government to more responsible debt management. Still the same scholar faulted the constitution's restrictions on indebtedness as in theory unduly restrictive and unrealistic, and in practice easily evaded and called for basic revisions.[8]

Counties remained the principal overseer of roads until after World War II, although throughout the twentieth century the Commonwealth and federal government absorbed an increasing share of road construction and maintenance. By 1923 a majority of counties had established either a county road engineer or road commission, but in at least fifty-three counties roads remained in a "deplorable" condition. Early in the century those counties retaining the traditional labor tax and overseer system continued to be bogged down in corruption, inefficiency, and mud. One county judge lamented that while his county had good roads in the summer, most people stayed at home in the winter.[9]

The framers of the fourth constitution perpetuated still another deficiency of county government, its nineteenth-century condition of headlessness. The delegates did not even debate the issue of whether to give a single county officer, presumably the county judge, supervisory power over other county officials and county business generally, and observers of county government seemed not to worry about the question either. Twentieth-century commentators began to illuminate the problem, conceding that in some counties there might occasionally be a de facto leader of government whose authority was measured by his political influence (usually the county judge, county attorney, or sheriff). But such authority, they contended, usually proved to be temporary and incomplete, and offered no substitute for constitutional power. Each county officer controlled the expenses of his office and made cost-cutting difficult, if not impossible. Increasingly, they called for creation of a central authority to provide more direction and coordination to county affairs.[10]

Twentieth-century critics of Kentucky's county system proposed other reforms, the most drastic of which involved elimination of large numbers of the counties themselves. Although proposals for county consolidation were advanced before the Great Depression, they grew more numerous during the period of economic holocaust, probably because of the tax savings that consolidation would arguably accomplish. In 1931 John Manning branded counties as obsolete in an age of sophisticated transportation and communications and called for the reduction of their number in Kentucky from 120 to twenty. Submitting that counties were afflicted with "misfit uniformity" because they were applied to rural and urban sections alike without regard to their special needs, Manning estimated that merger would save taxpayers over $2.5 million. The *Courier-Journal* quickly endorsed Manning's proposal, contending that consolidation would eliminate 4,000 useless jobs and wasteful duplication of numerous local governmental services. In a subsequent editorial, the newspaper charged that consolidation would curtail the "subversive" influence of Kentucky's "120 county political machines" which accounted for "practically every evil in [state] government from inequality of representation to inequality of taxation."[11]

Manning's proposal attracted support from other newspapers, several politicians (including, amazingly, some county officials), and the public at large. The state official most acquainted with the realities of county finances, state inspector and examiner Nat B. Sewell, endorsed consolidation in early 1933. Almost simultaneously, a reader of the *Courier-Journal* argued that elimination of many of Kentucky's counties would be a way to reduce the number of politicians whom he characterized as "parasites that are largely the cause of our mental distress and our financial decay." The *Bowling Green Times-Journal* and the *Carlisle County News* supported consolidation in the fall of 1935 largely because of hoped-for tax savings.[12]

But even its most ardent supporters realized the tremendous odds against the success of county consolidation. Aligned against such a change stood perhaps the most powerful collective political force in the Commonwealth, "120 entrenched courthouse cliques, and their families and friends." Often the product of these cliques or dependent upon them for reelection and necessary support, administrators and legislators in Frankfort feared political disaster if they tampered with the sanctity of county boundaries. Bolstering this opposition were hundreds of thousands of Kentuckians who derived special pride from their fierce county loyalties. Likewise most county newspapers opposed consolidation, allegedly because of their lucrative printing contracts with county governments. These detractors of county merger predicted the economic collapse of county seats destroyed by consolidation and attendant unemployment and loss of tax revenue. They argued that any tax savings derived from consolidation would be more than offset by the added expense of transportation to more remote county seats and by the cost of new courthouses needed to accommodate larger counties. Some even argued that it would be more difficult to enforce criminal laws if fewer counties existed.[13]

Concrete proposals to consolidate Kentucky's counties or to alter county government in substantial ways died quickly. In 1937 the legislature, faced with intense lobbying from county officers and their allies, defeated a proposed constitutional amendment permitting city-county merger. In 1954 a proposed joint resolution directing the Legislative Research Commission to study the feasibility of county merger languished in committee. Twelve years later the Constitution Revision Assembly in its proposed fifth constitution for the Commonwealth actually made it more difficult to consolidate counties by providing that voters had to approve such plans; nevertheless fears that the new charter somehow threatened the sanctity of Kentucky's counties helped produce its overwhelming defeat. Representing a rare glimmer of hope for reform of local government, Fayette County culminated several decades of cooperation with the city of Lexington by formally merging with that government in 1974 after voters overwhelmingly endorsed the legislatively sanctioned joinder.[14]

Kentucky's general failure to reform county government is not unique. In recent decades policymakers in more than a few states have stewed openly about the need to amalgamate counties or merge them with cities, but few have accomplished these objectives. The nation as a whole seems to delight more in the proliferation of local governmental units than in their abolition. In 1966 the Committee for Improvement of Management in Government reported that there were more than 80,000 such units, including over 3,000 counties and more than twenty times as many special districts (in Jefferson County alone there were 142 units). Of all local government, the county remains the most unreconstructed, constituting in the words of Gilbertson, the "dark continent of American politics." Although not alone in their refusal to tamper with their counties, Kentuckians arguably attach more significance to these constitutional creatures than any other Americans. For many the county seat remains the center of civilization commercially and socially; the county high school athletic teams inspire loyalty approaching patriotic fervor; the county courthouse constitutes a symbolic meetinghouse for both rich and poor; and the county continues to serve as the basis of the state's political machinery. In Kentucky, for better or for worse, counties are truly little kingdoms.[15]

NOTES

Chapter 1

1. *Official Report of the Proceedings and Debates in the Convention Assembled ... September, 1890 to ... Change the Constitution of Kentucky*, 4 vols. (Frankfort, 1890), 1: 402-3, hereafter cited as *Debates;* William W. Blair to L. M. Cox, 12 February 1856, Martin Cox Papers, King Library Special Collections, University of Kentucky, Microfilm.

2. *Debates*, 1: 328-29, 349, 394; *Louisville Courier-Journal*, 4, 5, 6 March 1869, 6 January 1890; *Covington Commonwealth*, 26 January 1880; *Louisville Daily Democrat*, 20 January 1867.

3. *Paris Western Citizen*, 29 March 1870; *Paris True Kentuckian*, 20 April, 28 December 1870; Lexington *Kentucky Gazette*, 3 April 1878.

4. *Montgomery County v. Menefee County Court*, 93 Kentucky Reports 33 (1892), hereafter cited as Ky.; *Bracken County Court v. Robertson County Court*, 69 Ky. 69 (1869); *Justices of Marshall County Court v. Justices of Calloway County Court*, 65 Ky. 93 (1867).

5. Leg. Doc. No. 10, *Kentucky Documents, 1851-1852*, pp. 427-526; Auditor's Report, Leg. Doc. No. 12, *Kentucky Documents, 1861*, 1: 241-348; *Stanford Interior Journal*, 21 March 1873; Auditor's Report, Leg. Doc. No. 19, *Kentucky Documents, 1891*, 2:166-69.

6. Frankfort *Kentucky Yeoman*, 21 June 1873, 28 August 1879; *Stanford Interior Journal*, 21 March 1873; *Barbourville Mountain Echo*, 5 December 1873; *Debates*, 1: 329-36.

7. *Debates*, 1: 343, 372-74, 392-96, 400-401.

8. Frankfort *Kentucky Yeoman*, 16 January 1872; *Hall v. Marshall*, 4 Kentucky Law Reporter 502 (1882), hereafter cited as Ky. L. Rep.

9. *Debates*, 1: 335, 393-94; *Falmouth Independent*, 4 October, 1 November 1877, 17 January 1878.

10. *Walters v. Richardson*, 14 Ky. L. Rep. 410 (1892); *Taylor v. Commonwealth*, 54 Ky. 11 (1854).

11. *Journal of the Senate of Kentucky, 1867-1868*, p. 267, hereafter cited as S. J.; *Journal of the House of Representatives of Kentucky, 1887-1888*, pp. 1544-46, hereafter cited as H. J.; S. J., *1887-1888*, pp. 134-37; Report on Rowan County, Leg. Doc. No. 3, *Kentucky Documents, 1888*, 1: 414.

12. *Maysville Bulletin*, 12 January 1871; Lexington *Kentucky Gazette*, 1 March 1876.
13. *Debates*, 1: 330-31, 337, 339, 341-43, 350, 354, 356; Constitution of 1891, sec. 63. Sections 64 and 65 restricted county boundary changes.
14. *Acts, 1879-1880*, Ch. 362; *Acts, 1877-1878*, Ch. 858; *Acts, 1871*, Ch. 1917; *Acts, 1867*, Ch. 2050.
15. *Maysville Bulletin*, 28 February 1878.
16. Charles Chauncey Binney, "Restrictions on Special and Local Legislation," *American Law Register*, n.s., 32 (1894): 613-32, 721-45, 816-57, 922-43, 1019-33, 1109-61; Lyman H. Cloe and Sumner Marcus, "Special and Local Legislation," *Kentucky Law Journal* 24 (May 1936): 355-56; *Maysville Bulletin*, 23 March 1876; *Debates*, 1: 395, 3: 3795; Frankfort *Kentucky Yeoman*, 8 December 1885; Bradley, *A Sketch of Granny Short's Barbecue and the General Statutes of Kentucky* (Louisville, 1879).
17. *Debates*, 1: 334, 395, 3: 3795-96, 3833, 4: 5759-60, 5763, 5766, 5769; *Stanford Interior Journal*, 16 January 1874; *Lexington Weekly Press*, 29 February 1888; Frankfort *Kentucky Yeoman*, 29 October 1885; Jefferson County Court Minute Book 31, p. 426 [all minute and order books on microfilm in King Library Special Collections, University of Kentucky, unless otherwise noted].
18. *H. J., 1859-1860*, pp. 480-81; *H. J., 1861-1863*, 1: 945, 972; *H. J., 1865*, p. 921; *H. J., 1873-1874*, pp. 165-66; *H. J., 1869*, pp. 27, 287-90; *H. J., 1871*, pp. 52-54.
19. *Frankfort Capital*, 17 March 1888; 7 October 1890; *Lexington Weekly Press*, 7 March 1888, 31 July 1889; *Louisville Courier-Journal*, 2 April 1890; *Debates*, 1: 85-86, 164, 168, 2: 2224-26, 3: 3472-73, 3795, 3989-4024, 4: 5277-79, 5755-57, 5767-68; Constitution of 1891, secs. 59-60, 139-42.
20. Lexington *Kentucky Gazette*, 14 July, 25, 29 December 1869, 8 January 1870; Lexington *Kentucky Statesman*, 16 July 1869.
21. *Lexington Weekly Press*, 4 March 1874, 10 April 1878, 4 November 1885.
22. *Acts, 1859-1860*, Ch. 1307; *Acts, 1867*, Ch. 1554.
23. *Acts, 1853-1854*, Ch. 299; *Acts, 1855-1856*, Ch. 272; Jefferson County Court Minute Book 27, pp. 3, 26-27, 37, 69, 160-61, 191-92, 293; *Louisville Daily Democrat*, 12 February 1868.
24. *Acts, 1851-1852*, Ch. 144; *Acts, 1857-1858*, Ch. 342; *Acts, 1861-1863*, Ch. 880; *Acts, 1885-1886*, Ch. 331.
25. *Acts, 1851-1852*, Ch. 157; *Acts, 1865-1866*, Ch. 22; *Acts, 1867*, Ch. 1408 and 1887; *Acts, 1867-1868*, Ch. 106; *Acts, 1869*, Ch. 1740-41; *Acts, 1869-1870*, Ch. 784; *Lexington Leader*, 1 July 1890.
26. *Acts, 1869*, Ch. 1285; Richard H. Stanton, ed., *Revised Statutes of Kentucky*, 2 vols. (Cincinnati, 1860), 2: 292-93; *Garrard County Court v. Boyle County Court*, 73 Ky. 208 (1874); *Grayson County Court v. Breckinridge County Court*, 7 Ky. L. Rep. 592 (1886).

Chapter 2

1. Lexington *Kentucky Gazette*, 30 June, 7, 14 July 1875; *Falmouth Independent*, 6 May 1878; *Paris True Kentuckian*, 17 December 1867.
2. For the powers of the county judges see Joshua F. Bullitt and John Feland, eds., *The General Statutes of Kentucky* (Louisville, 1888), pp. 277-78, 379-88, 719, 788, 790.
3. *Frankfort Commonwealth*, 15 May 1854; *Lexington Weekly Press*, 10 April 1878.
4. *Acts, 1865*, Ch. 749; Bullitt and Feland, *General Statutes* (1888), p. 383; *Kinnison v. Carpenter*, 71 Ky. 599 (1873); *Colter v. McIntire*, 74 Ky. 565 (1875).
5. Lexington *Kentucky Statesman*, 23 June 1871.
6. *Cynthiana News*, 9 April 1868; Danville *Kentucky Tribune*, 12 March 1852; *Gayle v. Owen County Court*, 83 Ky. 61 (1885); *Nepp v. Commonwealth*, 63 Ky. 546 (1866); *Anderson v. Commonwealth*, 76 Ky. 485 (1877).
7. *Lexington Observer and Reporter*, 29 July, 23 September 1857; *Frankfort Commonwealth*, 3 August, 23 September 1857; *Morgan v. Dudley*, 57 Ky. 693 (1857); McCracken County Order Book (1861-1869), pp. 91-93; Clark County Order Book (1864-1873), 2 November 1868; *Maysville Bulletin*, 13 May 1875.
8. *Frankfort Commonwealth*, 2 February 1854; *Barbourville Mountain Echo*, 9 January 1874; *Stanford Interior Journal*, 7 August, 30 October, 27 November 1874, 15 January 1875.
9. Lexington *Kentucky Gazette*, 19 June, 7 September 1878; *Lexington Leader*, 11 June 1890; *Maysville Bulletin*, 30 June 1870, 12 November 1874; *Lexington Weekly Press*, 30 May 1877; *Barbourville Mountain Echo*, 19 February 1875; Frankfort *Kentucky Yeoman*, 15 August 1876.
10. *Lexington Weekly Press*, 18 March 1874, 25 June 1884; *Lexington Observer and Reporter*, 2 September 1868; Lexington *Kentucky Gazette*, 26 September 1866; *Frankfort Capital*, 9 September 1890.
11. *Paris True Kentuckian*, 18 March 1874; *Cynthiana News*, 24 March 1870; *Maysville Bulletin*, 13 September 1877; *Lexington Weekly Press*, 10 April 1878; *Frankfort Commonwealth*, 15 May 1854; *Debates*, 3: 3481.
12. Bullitt and Feland, *General Statutes* (1888), pp. 1070-88; Frankfort *Kentucky Yeoman*, 28 March 1872; *London Mountain Echo*, 25 January 1884; *Paris True Kentuckian*, 29 July 1868.
13. *H. J., 1850-1851*, passim; *H. J., 1863-1864*, pp. 750-51; McCracken County Court Order Book (1861-1869), p. 142; *Paris True Bulletin*, 6 May 1868; *Acts, 1885-1886*, Ch. 500; *Acts, 1873-1874*, Ch. 88; *Acts, 1877-1878*, Ch. 169; *Acts, 1879-1880*, Ch. 63; Mt. Olivet *Robertson County Tribune*, 15 December 1881; *Louisville Courier-Journal*, 15 July 1890; *Hickman Courier*, 2 March, 4 May 1877; Bullitt and Feland, *General Statutes* (1888), p. 337; *H. J., 1877-1878*, pp. 886-87; *Acts, 1861-1863*, Ch. 825; *Barbourville Mountain Echo*, 30 April 1875; *Acts, 1861-1863*, Ch. 781; *Acts, 1875-1876*, Ch. 169; *Acts, 1863-1864*, Ch. 471.

14. Frankfort *Kentucky Yeoman*, 3 February 1871; *London Mountain Echo*, 25 January 1884.

15. *Commonwealth for the Use of Taylor v. Bradley's Executors*, 27 Ky. 209 (1830); *Commonwealth v. Reed*, 65 Ky. 618 (1866); *Commonwealth v. Williams*, 14 Ky. 335 (1823); *Forsythe v. Ellis*, 27 Ky. 298 (1830); *Thompson v. Commonwealth*, 10 Ky. L. Rep. 118 (1888); *Anderson v. Thompson*, 73 Ky. 132 (1873); *Griffith v. Commonwealth for the Use of Hughes*, 73 Ky. 281 (1874); *Acts, 1850-1851*, Ch. 214.

16. *Debates*, 3: 4035, 4114, 4126, 4162-63; Frankfort *Capital*, 10 December 1887; Auditor's Report, Leg. Doc. No. 1, *Kentucky Documents, 1880*, 3: x-xii; *Acts, 1881-1882*, Ch. 1384.

17. *Cynthiana News*, 5 June, 14, 21 August 1856, 16 December 1869; Mt. Olivet *Robertson County Tribune*, 23 March, 6 April 1882; Lexington *Kentucky Gazette*, 2 January 1875; *Paris True Kentuckian*, 11 May 1870.

18. Frankfort *Kentucky Yeoman*, 23 January 1872; *Debates*, 3: 4032, 4108-13; Constitution of 1850, Art. VI, sec. 4. The Constitution of 1891, sec. 99, gave sheriffs a four-year term, but made them ineligible "to re-election or to act as deputy for the succeeding term."

19. William B. Allen, *Kentucky Officer's Guide and Legal Handbook* ... (Louisville, 1860), pp. 201-15; *Lexington Weekly Press*, 6 August 1876.

20. Bullitt and Feland, *General Statutes* (1888), pp. 389-94, 435-36, 687, 689, 691, 983, 1211, 1214.

21. Robert M. Ireland, *The County Courts in Antebellum Kentucky* (Lexington, 1972), p. 166; *Lexington Weekly Press*, 12 June 1889.

22. *Georgetown Weekly Times*, 10 May 1871; *Paris True Kentuckian*, 13 March 1878; *Bardstown Herald*, 5 August 1852; *Maysville Republican*, 8 May 1875; *Lexington Weekly Press*, 17 April 1878; The Papers of Governor Beriah Magoffin, J. 1200, 1232, Kentucky Historical Society; County Judge John S. Girger to John W. Stevenson, The Papers of Governor John W. Stevenson, J. 1643; The Papers of Governor Luke P. Blackburn, J. 3162; Frankfort *Kentucky Yeoman*, 5 February 1859.

23. *H. J., 1851-1852*, pp. 228-29; *S. J., 1851-1852*, pp. 428-29; *H. J., 1853-1854*, p. 41; *S. J., 1853-1854*, pp. 60, 84, 136-38; *H. J., 1855-1856*, pp. 63, 226, 317-18; *H. J., 1859-1860*, pp. 93, 163; *S. J., 1859-1860*, p. 72; *S. J., 1867-1868*, pp. 628-29; *H. J., 1867-1868*, p. 708; *S. J., 1869*, pp. 653-54; *Acts, 1873-1874*, Ch. 160; *Acts, 1883-1884*, Ch. 687; Frankfort *Kentucky Yeoman*, 20 February 1873. Other statutes made the civil jurisdiction of justices of the peace even more uneven. Bullitt and Feland, *General Statutes* (1888), pp. 392-93.

24. *Lexington Observer and Reporter*, 19 June 1867; *Lexington Weekly Press*, 29 May 1878; *Cynthiana News*, 23 August 1855; Frankfort *Kentucky Yeoman*, 27 January 1881; *Debates*, 3: 4123.

25. Frankfort *Kentucky Yeoman*, 20 February 1873; *Debates*, 3: 4061, 4121, 4181-84; *Paris Western Citizen*, 13 February 1872.

26. *Louisville Courier-Journal*, 15 February 1891.

27. *Debates*, 3: 4183-84; Frankfort *Kentucky Yeoman*, 25 March 1873; Falmouth *Independent*, 3 January 1878; *Lexington Weekly Press*, 12 November 1890; *London Mountain Echo*, 14 September 1883.

28. *Georgetown Weekly Times*, 17 July 1872; Lexington *Kentucky Statesman*, 20 August 1869; *Louisville Courier-Journal*, 20 January 1891; *Louisville Evening Post*, 14, 17 May 1879; *Ayars* v. *Cox*, 73 Ky. 201 (1874); *Bullitt* v. *Clement*, 55 Ky. 193 (1855); *Pepper* v. *Mayes*, 81 Ky. 673 (1884); *Bryant* v. *Rubee*, 1 Ky. L. Rep. 57 (1880); *Revill* v. *Pettit*, 60 Ky. 314 (1860); *Maysville Bulletin*, 18 May 1871.

29. Frankfort *Kentucky Yeoman*, 20 February 1873; *Louisville Courier-Journal*, 15 February 1891.

30. Ireland, *The County Courts*, pp. 91-92; *Louisville Courier-Journal*, 17 March, 16 May 1890; *Frankfort Commonwealth*, 2 February 1854; *Frankfort Capital*, 2 May 1885; Mt. Olivet *Robertson County Tribune*, 24 June 1880.

31. Bullitt and Feland, *General Statutes* (1888), pp. 397, 495, 1065-70; Frankfort *Kentucky Yeoman*, 8, 21, 28 October, 16 November 1869; *Acts, 1851-1852*, Ch. 271; *Acts, 1867*, Ch. 1309; *Debates*, 4: 5412-13; *Talbott's Devisees* v. *Hooser*, 75 Ky. 408 (1876).

32. Bullitt and Feland, *General Statutes* (1888), pp. 179, 457; *Frankfort Commonwealth*, 2 February 1854; *Acts, 1861-1863*, Ch. 1065.

33. Frankfort *Kentucky Yeoman*, 28 October 1869; cf. *Maysville Bulletin*, 23 July 1874.

34. Bullitt and Feland, *General Statutes* (1888), pp. 177-78, 180-82, 1038, 1058.

35. *Debates*, 2: 1681-86, 1694, 3: 4029, 4051, 4056, 4060-61, 4071, 4170-71; *Frankfort Capital*, 10 March 1891; *Louisville Evening Post*, 25 July 1878; *London Mountain Echo*, 9 April 1886.

36. Bullitt and Feland, *General Statutes* (1888), pp. 377, 464-65, 802, 805-6, 1015-16; *Debates*, 3: 3465.

37. *Frankfort Capital*, 21 February 1886; Lexington *Kentucky Gazette*, 2 July 1870; Lexington *Kentucky Statesman*, 20 August 1858, 25 January 1859; Frankfort *Kentucky Yeoman*, 6, 18 November 1858, 25 January 1859; *Batman* v. *Megowan*, 58 Ky. 533 (1859).

38. *London Mountain Echo*, 28 January 1876, 4 July 1879; *Hite* v. *Whitley County Court*, 12 Ky. L. Rep. 764 (1891); *Commonwealth* v. *Mitchell*, 66 Ky. 30 (1867); *McBride* v. *Commonwealth*, 67 Ky. 331 (1868).

39. Bullitt and Feland, *General Statutes* (1888), pp. 334, 933, 1053-55; *Acts, 1850-1851*, Ch. 262; *Acts, 1863-1864*, Ch. 124; *Debates*, 3: 4119-20, 4123, 4182; *Hickman Courier*, 20 January, 10 February 1882; Frankfort *Kentucky Yeoman*, 28 August 1879; *Frankfort Commonwealth*, 13 August 1858; *Paris True Kentuckian*, 11 April 1877.

40. Bullitt and Feland, *General Statutes* (1888), p. 326; *Acts, 1863-1864*, Ch. 351.

41. *Paris Western Citizen*, 29 March, 5 April 1870; Lexington *Kentucky*

Statesman, 10, 14 May 1872; *Louisville Courier*, 3, 5 August 1854; *Maysville Bulletin*, 14 July 1870; *Debates*, 3: 4124. On 24 January 1926 the *Courier-Journal* reported that "for the first time in sixty years Barren County has a coroner."

42. Richard H. Stanton, *A Practical Treatise on the . . . Powers and Duties of Justices of the Peace* [etc.] . . . (Cincinnati, 1875), pp. 750-57.

43. *Louisville Courier-Journal*, 26 July 1891; Frankfort *Kentucky Yeoman*, 5 August 1882; Mt. Olivet *Robertson County Tribune*, 24 June 1880.

44. *Falmouth Independent*, 6, 13 June 1878; *Louisville Evening Post*, 5, 15 October 1878; Board v. Head, 33 Ky. 489 (1835); *Louisville Courier-Journal*, 26 January 1885.

45. Bullitt and Feland, *General Statutes* (1888), p. 1226; *Lexington Weekly Press*, 30 April, 15 October 1879.

46. *Acts, 1869-1870*, Ch. 831; *Acts, 1885-1886*, Ch. 75; *Acts, 1857-1858*, Ch. 602; *Debates*, 3: 4163; Montgomery County v. Mitchell, 5 Ky. L. Rep. 249 (1883); Bullitt and Feland, *General Statutes* (1888), p. 970.

47. Atchison, County Judge v. Lucas, 83 Ky. 451 (1885); Fayette County Court Order Book (1880-1883), p. 364 (Fayette County Courthouse, Lexington); *Acts, 1887-1888*, Ch. 944.

Chapter 3

1. For example see Bullitt and Feland, *General Statutes* (1888), pp. 507, 511; Stanton, *Revised Statutes*, 1: 431.

2. *Louisville Journal*, 12, 22 May 1851. See for example *Frankfort Commonwealth*, 27 May 1851.

3. Frankfort *Kentucky Yeoman*, 10, 12, 15 August 1854; 7, 13 August 1858; *Louisville Journal*, 9 August 1854; *Louisville Daily Democrat*, 4-18 August 1858.

4. Lexington *Kentucky Statesman*, 30 April 1851, 8 August 1854, 23 February, 23, 31 July 1858; *Frankfort Commonwealth*, 12 April, 19 May, 14 July, 2, 4, 11 August 1858, 6 April 1859; Frankfort *Kentucky Yeoman*, 25 April, 31 July, 3 August 1858.

5. O. P. Hogan to B. Magoffin, 21 June 1862; Papers of Gov. Magoffin, J. 1234; *Louisville Journal*, 4-10 August 1862.

6. *Louisville Journal*, 7 August 1866; Frankfort *Kentucky Yeoman*, 14 August 1866.

7. *Louisville Courier-Journal*, 1-10 August 1870; *Louisville Daily Commercial*, 2-24 August 1870.

8. Lexington *Kentucky Statesman*, 25 June, 5 July, 6 August 1872; Lexington *Kentucky Gazette*, 26, 29 June 1872, 5 August 1874; Fayette County Court Order Book (1869-1873), p. 586, Court Order Book (1873-1876), pp. 43, 151 (Fayette County Courthouse, Lexington).

9. *Maysville Bulletin*, 23 July 1874; *Louisville Courier-Journal*, 4-11 August 1874; *Stanford Interior Journal*, 27 March, 3 April, 24 July, 16 October 1874; *Barbourville Mountain Echo*, 19 June, 7 August 1874; *Louisville Daily Commercial*, 4-20 August 1874.

10. *Louisville Courier-Journal*, 6-12 August 1878; *Louisville Daily Commercial*, 6-28 August 1878.

11. *Louisville Courier-Journal*, 8-12 August 1882, 3-10 August 1886; *Louisville Daily Commercial*, 8-20 August 1882, 3-18 August 1886.

12. *Louisville Courier-Journal*, 5-10 August 1890.

13. *Boone County Recorder* as reported in the *Falmouth Independent*, 7 February 1878; *Louisville Courier-Journal*, 8 August 1878; *Lexington Kentucky Gazette*, 16 February, 10 July 1878, 26 February 1879.

14. *Louisville Courier-Journal*, 11 August 1874, 7, 8 August 1878, 8 August 1882, 3 August 1886; *Maysville Bulletin*, 30 July 1874, 7 February 1878; *Maysville Republican*, 6, 13 June 1874, 27 June 1878; *Falmouth Independent*, 7 February 1878.

15. Ireland, *The County Courts*, pp. 87-95; *Acts, 1850-1851*, Ch. 617 (ch. 4); *Oldham's Trustee v. Hume*, 11 Kentucky Opinions 779 (1882), hereafter cited as Ky. Op.; *Montgomery County Court v. Mitchell*, 5 Ky. L. Rep. 249 (1883).

16. *Louisville Courier-Journal*, 8 August 1882; Report on Rowan County, Leg. Doc. No. 3, *Kentucky Documents, 1888*, 1: 484-85; *Lexington Leader*, 2 July, 3 August 1890; see, for example, *Deskins v. Phillip's Adm'r.*, 11 Ky. L. Rep. 485 (1889).

17. *Louisville Courier-Journal*, 8, 9 August 1882, 3 August 1886; *Barbourville Mountain Echo*, 31 July 1874.

18. *Louisville Courier-Journal*, 6, 8 August 1878, 5 August 1890.

19. Frankfort *Kentucky Yeoman*, 10 August 1854, 3 August 1858; *Lexington Leader*, 1, 5 August 1890; John L. Scott to Brutus J. Clay, 5 August 1863, Brutus Clay Papers, King Library Special Collections, University of Kentucky, Microfilm M-227.

20. *Frankfort Commonwealth*, 28, 30 July 1858; Frankfort *Kentucky Yeoman*, 7 August 1858.

21. *Lexington Weekly Press*, 8 July 1874, 13 June 1877.

22. *Cynthiana News*, 8 June, 6, 20 July 1871; *Maysville Bulletin*, 30 July 1874, 8 August 1878.

23. *Hickman Courier*, 7 June 1878; *Cynthiana News*, 25 July 1872; *Maysville Bulletin*, 30 July 1874, 8 August 1878; *Maysville Republican*, 31 July 1875. Cynics might brand cliques and rings as mythical creations of "out" politicians, but courthouse politicians did influence the state's political behavior. Although county officers did not dominate county political machines after 1850 as much as they had before, they nonetheless continued to be influential. Candidates for elected office especially catered to the sheriff who remained the principal elections officer and who could exercise great leverage at the polls with his pockets crammed

with unexecuted judgments, summonses, and other intimidating judicial orders. Often the balance of political power within a county shifted according to which party controlled the sheriffalty. County judges and clerks also frequently maintained prominent positions within the local party hierarchy and some were even declared "political bosses." In many ways Kentucky's counties constituted not only her governmental foundation, but her political base as well.

24. *Paris True Kentuckian*, 7 June 1866, 3 March 1868, 15, 22 May, 7 July 1869, 10 May 1870, 25 March 1874.

25. Lexington *Kentucky Gazette*, 16 January, 8 February, 2 December 1868, 12, 19 January, 19 February 1870, 8, 11, 15, 18, 29 May, 8 June, 10 August 1878, 12 February 1879; *Lexington Weekly Press*, 25 March 1874, 6 August 1876, 28 January 1880, 5 October 1881, 14 May, 2 July 1884, 11 September 1889; Frankfort *Kentucky Yeoman*, 6 April 1869, 6 June 1876, 1 January, 12 March 1878, 3 February 1880; *Hickman Courier*, 8 September 1876, 14 June, 19 July 1878.

26. *Maysville Bulletin*, 10 March 1870, 6 November 1873, 28 March, 11 April, 20 June, 4, 25 July, 8 August 1878; *Maysville Republican*, 31 July 1875, 23 June 1877.

27. *Maysville Bulletin,* 6 November 1873; *Stanford Interior Journal,* 17 May 1872; *Paris True Kentuckian*, 7 July 1869; *Lexington Weekly Press,* 15 August 1877.

28. *Falmouth Independent*, 28 March, 9, 16 May, 20 June 1878.

29. *Maysville Bulletin*, 2, 25 July, 8 August 1878.

30. *Cynthiana News*, 5 March, 6 August, 10 September 1868, 6, 20 January, 28 April 1870, 8 June, 2, 20 July 1871, 4 April 1872, 27 March, 3 April 1873.

31. *Louisville Courier-Journal*, 4 April 1890; *Acts, 1879-1880*, Ch. 1018; *Acts, 1881-1882*, Ch. 336; *Acts, 1885-1886*, Ch. 772; *Acts, 1887-1888*, Ch. 689; *Acts, 1889-1890*, Ch. 448; *Acts, 1891-1893*, Ch. 65, Art. XII. Counties securing special legislation cited above were Harrison, Bourbon, Campbell, Kenton, Nicholas, Robertson, Greenup, Boone, Lewis, Woodford, Jessamine, Simpson, Franklin, Bracken, Pendleton, and Magoffin.

Chapter 4

1. *Acts, 1861-1863*, Chs. 563, 564.

2. G. A. Flournoy to Governor Magoffin, 22 May 1862, Papers of Gov. Magoffin, J. 1234; Ezekiel Hobbs et al. to Magoffin, 19 April 1862, Papers of Gov. Magoffin, J. 1235.

3. *Acts, 1861-1863*, Ch. 392, 693, 699; *Acts, 1863-1864*, Chs. 65, 537; *H. J., 1861-1863*, p. 673.

4. McCracken County Court Order Book (1861-1869), pp. 20, 22-23, 25, 97, 124; *Acts, 1865*, Ch. 1631; see, for example, *Acts, 1861-1863*, Ch. 224, and McCracken County Court Order Book (1861-1869), p. 121.

5. *Acts, 1861-1863*, Chs. 193, 208; *Acts, 1863-1864*, Ch. 334; *Acts, 1865*, Ch. 688.

6. Frankfort *Kentucky Yeoman*, 24 August 1861; *Acts, 1861-1863*, Ch. 610; E. Merton Coulter, *Civil War and Readjustment in Kentucky* (Chapel Hill, N.C., 1926), p. 196; *Acts, 1865*, Chs. 607, 617, 777, 965. The Court of Appeals ruled that the bounty tax statutes were unconstitutional except as they applied to adult males who benefited from them. *Ferguson* v. *Landram*, 64 Ky. 548 (1866), 68 Ky. 230 (1868).

7. *Acts, 1861-1863*, Ch. 346; McCracken County Order Book (1861-1869), pp. 80-81, 83, 112, 130, 182, 231; *Leeman* v. *Hinton*, 62 Ky. 38 (1863); *Mershon* v. *Ballew*, Leg. Doc. No. 10, *Kentucky Documents, 1865*, 1: 3-21.

8. Major General O. O. Howard to Assistant Commissioners, 4 October 1865, *Executive Documents No. 50 to 72, 1st Sess., 39th Cong.;* Brigadier General Clinton B. Fisk, Circular to Bureau Agents, 10 October 1865, ibid.

9. *Acts, 1865-1866*, Ch. 621; Brigadier General John Ely to Major General Jefferson C. Davis, 15 August 1866, Letters Sent (28 March 1866 to 1 September 1866), pp. 252-53, Record Group 105, Freedmen's Bureau Records, National Archives; Report for January 1867, Letters Sent (February to July 1867), pp. 9-10.

10. See monthly reports in Freedmen's Bureau Letters Sent (Kentucky), Record Group 105, National Archives; Monthly Report, November 1866, Russell, Wayne and Adair counties, Record Group 105, ibid.

11. Brig. Gen'l John Ely to Willis Street, 19 June 1866, Letters Sent (March to September 1866), p. 142; Levi F. Burnett to Mrs. Green Mudd, 4 May 1866, ibid., p. 56; Burnett to Mrs. Caroline Murphy, 20 May 1866, ibid., pp. 67-68; Burnett to Jack Dickinson, 9 May 1866, ibid., p. 66; Ely to N. R. Black, *circa* June 1866, ibid., p. 144.

12. Levi F. Burnett to John L. Peyton, 1 September 1866, Letters Sent (March to September 1866), p. 288; Monthly Report for Cumberland, Clinton, and Monroe counties, August 1866, ibid.; *Paris True Kentuckian*, 17 January 1867. The Bourbon County Court Order Book nowhere refers to Hawes's ruling. Bourbon County Court Order Book (1866-1870), passim (Bourbon County Courthouse, Paris).

13. Other counties sampled were Barren, Clark, Henderson, Henry, Hickman, Jefferson, McCracken, and Warren; microfilm of order books is located in King Library Special Collections, University of Kentucky.

14. John Ely to Brig. Gen. Sidney Burbank, 13 March 1867, Letters Sent (10 February to 9 July 1867), p. 78; Ben Runkle to Lt. A. Benson Brown, 30 October 1867, Letters Sent (29 October 1867 to 24 February 1868), pp. 4-5; Burbank to Howard, 13 January 1868, Letters Sent (29 October 1867 to 24 February 1868), pp. 215-25; Federal Circuit Court Order Book C, 20 September 1866 to 11 June 1868 (Western District, Kentucky), Federal Archives and Records Center, Chicago, pp. 211, 252, 271, 306, 314, 323, 330-31, 360, 417, 439, 448, 457; Federal Circuit Court Order Book D (12 June 1868 to 15 November 1869), passim.

15. Fisk's Circular to Bureau Agents; *Acts, 1865-1866*, Ch. 636; *Acts, 1867*, Ch. 1913; *Acts, 1867-1868*, Ch. 56; John Ely to A. C. Swartzwalder, 2 June 1866, Letters Sent (March to September 1866), p. 120; Monthly Report for December 1866 for Barren, Hart, Green and Metcalfe counties, Record Group 105.

16. Col. Benjamin P. Runkle to James Speed, 1 November 1867, Letters Sent (October 1867 to February 1868), pp. 9-10; Runkle to Brig. Gen. Sidney Burbank, 21 December 1867, ibid., pp. 131-32; Runkle to Burbank, 13 March 1868, Letters Sent (February 1868 to December 1868), p. 64; Runkle to Burbank, 10 April 1868, ibid., p. 170.

17. Barren County Court Order Book (1864-1870), pp. 204, 296, 325, 343, 376, 404, 435-36, 445, 462, 472; Boyle County Court Order Book (1859-1868), pp. 527, 539, 567, 618; Christian County Court Order Book (1862-1867), pp. 413, 458, 478, 485-86, 489; ibid. (1867-1870), pp. 41, 45, 64-65, 85, 126, 194-95, 199-200; Clark County Court Order Book (1863-1874), pp. 153, 167, 171-72, 174, 178-79, 183; Henderson County Court Order Book (1866-1871), pp. 22, 53-57, 131, 228, 323-28; Henry County Court Order Book (1861-1868), pp. 427, 479, 486, 513, 642-44, 685; Hickman County Court Order Book (1864-1869), pp. 255, 263, 336; ibid. (1868-1874), p. 20; Jefferson County Court Order Book (1867-1868), pp. 386, 584-85; McCracken County Court Order Book (1861-1869), pp. 265, 349, 427; Warren County Court Order Book (1867-1869), pp. 224-25; ibid. (1869-1871), pp. 24-29, 31, 229, 240-41.

Chapter 5

1. *New York Times* as reported in *London Mountain Echo*, 24 August 1883; *Debates*, 2: 1685, 3: 4041, 4170, 4680.

2. Richard Maxwell Brown, "The American Vigilante Tradition," in Hugh Davis Graham and Ted Robert Gurr, eds., *Violence in America: Historical and Comparative Perspectives*, 2 vols. (Washington, D.C., 1969), 1: 175-76; Allen W. Trelease, *White Terror: The Ku Klux Klan Conspiracy and Southern Reconstruction* (New York, 1971), pp. 89-90, 124.

3. Trelease, *White Terror*, pp. 125, 280-84; *H. J., 1870-1871*, pp. 15-16; *H. J., 1871-1872*, pp. 702-7; *Acts, 1873*, Ch. 767; *New York Times*, 4 December 1868; *Lexington Weekly Press*, 22, 29 November 1874, 23 January 1878; *London Mountain Echo*, 13 September 1889.

4. *Falmouth Independent*, 13 April 1877; *Maysville Bulletin*, 25 October 1877; *H. J., 1877-1878*, pp. 62-63; Lexington *Kentucky Gazette*, 26 January 1878; *Covington Commonwealth*, 30 December 1879; Frankfort *Kentucky Yeoman*, 3 August 1882; *London Mountain Echo*, 24 August 1883; *H. J., 1889-1890*, pp. 32-35.

5. *Lexington Weekly Press*, 1, 4, 18 December 1878; *Louisville Evening Post*, 6 December 1878; Harold Wilson Coates, *Stories of Kentucky Feuds* (Knoxville, 1923), pp. 95-115.

6. Sources for the Rowan County feud include *Lexington Weekly Press*, 18 March, 1, 8 April 1885, 27 January 1886, 19 January 1887; Frankfort *Kentucky Yeoman*, 14 April 1885; *Louisville Courier-Journal*, 16 July 1885, 22 August 1886; Report on Rowan County, Leg. Doc. No. 3, *Kentucky Documents, 1888*, 1: 3-23, 94-95, 98, 178, 385-86, 460-61, 464-65, 489-90; *H. J., 1887-1888*, pp. 32-35; *S. J., 1887-1888*, pp. 908-14.

7. *Lexington Weekly Press*, 26 February 1879; Sam E. Hill to Governor S. B. Buckner, 14 November 1888, Adjutant-General's Report, Leg. Doc. No. 17, *Kentucky Documents, 1889*, 4: 36-38; J. M. Sohan to Hill, 27 November 1889, ibid., pp. 38-45; Hill to Buckner, 13 November 1889, ibid., pp. 45-49.

8. *Debates*, 1: 393-94, 400-401; *Louisville Courier-Journal*, 5, 30 June, 15 July 1885; *New York Times*, 26 December 1878; *Lexington Leader*, 20 July 1890.

9. Joshua F. Bullitt and John Feland, eds., *General Statutes* (Frankfort, 1877), pp. 300, 309; Bullitt and Feland, *General Statutes* (1888), pp. 377-79, 391; Stanton, *A Practical Treatise* (1875), pp. 435-36, 438, 487-92; *Acts, 1885-1886*, Ch. 682.

10. Bullitt and Feland, *General Statutes* (1888), pp. 287, 326, 377, 464-65, 803, 1015-16; *Maysville Republican*, 11 March 1876; *Paris True Kentuckian*, 26 December 1877; *Acts, 1855-1856*, Ch. 328; *Acts, 1869*, Ch. 1455; *Acts, 1869-1870*, Ch. 902.

11. *Maysville Bulletin*, 25 August 1870; *H. J., 1871-1872*, pp. 31, 33, 706-7; *H. J., 1873-1874*, pp. 21-24; *Falmouth Independent*, 12 April 1877; *New York Times* as reported in the *London Mountain Echo*, 24 August 1883; *H. J., 1889-1890*, pp. 32-35.

12. Frankfort *Kentucky Yeoman*, 22 March 1872; *Lexington Observer and Reporter*, 22 September 1869; Lexington *Kentucky Gazette*, 12 January 1878; *Winchester Sun*, 11, 14 March 1879; *Frankfort Capital*, 23 August 1884.

13. *Frankfort Commonwealth*, 13 September 1867; Mt. Olivet *Robertson County Tribune*, 25 October 1883; Stanton, *A Practical Treatise*, pp. 760-61; Frankfort *Kentucky Yeoman*, 7 December 1882; *Owensboro Monitor* as reported in the *Yeoman*, 20 February 1873.

14. Lexington *Kentucky Gazette*, 11 December 1872; *Debates*, 2: 1686, 1688, 3: 4043-45, 4048-49, 4058-59.

15. *Louisville Democrat*, 14 February 1868; *Falmouth Independent*, 13 December 1877; *H. J., 1873*, p. 16; Lexington *Kentucky Gazette*, 8 September 1877.

16. *Louisville Evening Post*, 4 February 1879; *Paris True Kentuckian*, 26 December 1877.

17. *New York Times* as reported in *London Mountain Echo*, 24 August 1883; *H. J., 1881-1882*, pp. 36-37.

18. Bullitt and Feland, *General Statutes* (1888), pp. 181-85, 624, 629,

631-32, 636-38, 710-11; *H. J.*, *1871-1872*, p. 27; *H. J.*, *1873*, p. 17; Auditor's Report, Leg. Doc. No. 3, *Kentucky Documents*, *1889*, 2: vi-vii, 144.

19. *H. J.*, *1879-1880*, pp. 40-41; Bullitt and Feland, *General Statutes* (1888), pp. 255-57; Auditor's Report, Leg. Doc. No. 6, *Kentucky Documents*, *1885*, 1: ix-xi; Auditor's Report, Leg. Doc. No. 13, *Kentucky Documents*, *1887*, 1: v.

20. *Louisville Courier-Journal*, 5 June 1885; *H. J.*, *1885-1886*, p. 24.

21. *H. J.*, *1871-1872*, p. 249; Frankfort *Kentucky Yeoman*, 19 January 1871, 11 February 1873; *Falmouth Independent*, 30 August 1877; *Lexington Weekly Press*, 26 January 1877, 13 February 1878.

22. *H. J.*, *1873*, p. 16; Lexington *Kentucky Gazette*, 26 January 1877, 19 March 1879; *Lexington Weekly Press*, 6 February 1878; Frankfort *Kentucky Yeoman*, 1 June 1880; *Paris True Kentuckian*, 26 December 1877.

23. *H. J.*, *1871-1872*, p. 33; *Acts*, *1873*, Ch. 767; *H. J.*, *1889-1890*, p. 34.

24. *H. J.*, *1873-1874*, pp. 19-21; *H. J.*, *1889-1890*, p. 34; *H. J.*, *1871-1872*, p. 33.

25. *Acts*, *1855-1856*, Ch. 98; *Acts*, *1857-1858*, Ch. 511; *Acts*, *1859-1860*, Ch. 970; *Acts*, *1861-1863*, Ch. 882; *Acts*, *1865*, Ch. 1758; Lincoln County Court Order Book (1857-1865), passim.

26. *Acts*, *1869-1870*, Ch. 696; *Acts*, *1873-1874*, Ch. 256; *Acts*, *1875-1876*, Ch. 38; Jefferson County Court Order Book (1884-1885), pp. 65, 171-72, 504. Order books of the following counties were examined: Adair, Bell, Boone, Breathitt, Bullitt, Butler, Marion, Pike, Rowan, Muhlenberg, Nelson, Ohio, Wayne, Union, Russell, Green, Henderson, Hickman, and Campbell. Microfilm of order books is located in King Library Special Collections, University of Kentucky.

27. *Acts*, *1867*, Ch. 1876; *Lexington Weekly Press*, 21 May, 18 June 1876; Lexington *Kentucky Gazette*, 29 December 1877.

28. *Acts*, *1877-1878*, Ch. 266; Fayette County Court of Claims Book (1874-1883), passim; ibid. (1884-1891), passim (Kentucky State Archives, Frankfort).

29. *Acts*, *1885-1886*, Chs. 97, 99, 1281; *Acts*, *1889-1890*, Ch. 1844; Fayette County Court of Claims Book (1884-1891), pp. 368-69, 374; Campbell County Court Order Book (1883-1887), passim; ibid. (1887-1893), passim; Kenton County Order Book (1886-1890), passim.

Chapter 6

1. Frankfort *Kentucky Yeoman*, 28 April 1868; Lexington *Kentucky Statesman*, 9 February 1869; *Paris True Kentuckian*, 10 January 1872.

2. Lexington *Kentucky Statesman*, 12 April 1872; Lexington *Kentucky Gazette*, 22 April 1871, 29 March 1876, 19 February 1879; *Lexington*

Weekly Press, 26 September 1877; James Lane Allen, "County Court Day in Kentucky," *Harper's Magazine* 79 (August 1889): 383-97.

3. Lexington *Observer and Reporter,* 27 October 1869; Lexington *Kentucky Gazette,* 9 June 1880; Lexington *Weekly Press,* 20 December 1885.

4. Lexington *Kentucky Gazette,* 11 July 1866; Lexington *Kentucky Statesman,* 15 February 1853, 14 April 1857, 10 April 1860, 9 April 1867, 15 December 1868; *Lexington Observer and Reporter,* 11 February 1857, 15 September 1868, 10 February, 25 August, 16 October 1869.

5. Lexington *Kentucky Statesman,* 15 December 1868, 23 November 1869; *Lexington Observer and Reporter,* 10 February, 3 April, 16 October 1869; Lexington *Kentucky Gazette,* 7 April 1869.

6. *Lexington Observer and Reporter,* 16 October 1869; Lexington *Kentucky Statesman,* 11 January 1870; *Paris True Kentuckian,* 14 February 1872; Lexington *Kentucky Gazette,* 10 July 1878; *Lexington Weekly Press,* 2 April 1879.

7. *Acts of the Kentucky Legislature to Incorporate the City of Lexington and Ordinances Passed in Pursuance Thereof . . .* , sec. 304 (Lexington, 1882); Lexington *Daily Press,* 17 September 1882; *Lexington Weekly Press,* 20 December 1885; Lexington *Kentucky Gazette,* 14 November 1888.

8. Lexington *Kentucky Reporter,* 21 April 1830; *Lexington Observer and Reporter,* 11 April 1833, 10 April 1861, 11 April 1866, 10 April 1872; Lexington *Kentucky Gazette,* 15 April 1870; Lexington *Kentucky Statesman,* 9 April 1867, 14 April 1868; Frankfort *Kentucky Yeoman,* 4 April 1871; *Lexington Daily Press,* 11 April 1871, 14 April 1874, 12 April 1881; *Lexington Morning Transcript,* 15 April 1890; *Lexington Herald,* 14 April 1896, 9 April 1907, 7 April 1916, 10 April 1917, 1 July 1937.

9. Allen, "County Court Day," p. 394.

10. *Lexington Daily Press,* 29 September 1882; Frankfort *Kentucky Yeoman,* 4 May 1879, 6 February, 8 October 1872; *Lexington Observer and Reporter,* 11 February, 10 October 1857, 15 September 1868; Lexington *Kentucky Statesman,* 15 February 1853; *Lexington Weekly Press,* 9 May 1888.

11. *Lexington Weekly Press,* 25 March 1874, 10 July 1889; *Lexington Observer and Reporter,* 7 February 1856, 11 March 1857, 11 November 1863; *Cynthiana News,* 15 April 1869; *Wade v. Covington City National Bank,* 2 Ky. L. Rep. 231 (1881).

12. *New York Times,* 3 October 1874. In the opinion of the *Covington Commonwealth* (9 January 1880), "a man without a title in Kentucky is nowhere, and in public affairs, no account."

13. Lexington *Kentucky Gazette,* 26 February, 9 April 1873.

14. *Frankfort Roundabout,* 6 December 1890; *Lexington Weekly Press,* 16 July 1876, 14 January, 16 December 1885; Lexington *Kentucky Gazette,* 7 April 1869; *Lexington Observer and Reporter,* 16 October

1869; James Lane Allen, "County Court Day," pp. 384, 386, 388, 393; *Paris True Kentuckian*, 8 November 1866; *Cynthiana News*, 12 October 1854, 16 May 1867; Mt. Olivet *Robertson County Tribune*, 22 January 1880, 12 December 1882; Frankfort *Kentucky Yeoman*, 27 January 1881.

15. Lexington *Kentucky Statesman*, 3 May 1853, 20 August 1861, 7 July 1881; *Cynthiana News*, 16 June 1853; Frankfort *Kentucky Yeoman*, 17 January 1866, 28 July 1868, 7 April 1874; *Frankfort Commonwealth*, 30 May 1859, 16 July 1860, 1 May 1863, 18 April 1864; *Lexington Observer and Reporter*, 30 April 1870; *Frankfort Capital*, 26 November 1887, 30 June 1891; *Louisville Courier-Journal*, 14 July 1891; *Lexington Weekly Press*, 23 January 1878; John A. Williams to Roderick Perry, 28 September 1876, Perry Family Papers, Box 3 (70M11), King Library Special Collections, University of Kentucky.

16. William H. Townsend, *Lincoln and His Wife's Home Town* (Indianapolis, Ind., 1929), pp. 148-51; J. Winston Coleman, *Slavery Times in Kentucky* (Chapel Hill, N.C., 1940), pp. 115-19, 146; *Lexington Observer and Reporter*, 16 August 1848, 13 June 1849; Allen, "County Court Day," p. 396.

17. Lexington *Kentucky Gazette*, 13 March 1869, 8 June 1870; *Cynthiana News*, 15 June 1854, 16 June 1870.

18. *Cynthiana News*, 14 January 1869, 6, 27 April, 27 July 1871; Bullitt and Feland, *General Statutes* (1888), p. 370; Frankfort *Kentucky Yeoman*, 28 April 1868; Lexington *Kentucky Gazette*, 2 February 1870, 29 January 1873; Lexington *Kentucky Statesman*, 11 February 1870.

19. *London Mountain Echo*, 29 June 1877; Mt. Olivet *Robertson County Tribune*, 22 January 1880; *Paris True Kentuckian*, 14 January 1868; *Cynthiana News*, 9 June 1853; Frankfort *Kentucky Yeoman*, 3 December 1872; *Lexington Observer and Reporter*, 11 December 1872; *Stanford Interior Journal*, 26 September 1873, 18 December 1874; *Lexington Weekly Press*, 14 January 1885; B. O. Gaines, *History of Scott County*, 2 vols. (Georgetown, Ky., 1906), 1: 204-5.

20. *Louisville Courier-Journal*, 22 January 1928, 22 February 1940, 10 April 1950.

Chapter 7

1. Constitution of 1850, Art. II, secs. 35, 36, 40; *Acts, 1871*, Ch. 1409; *Acts, 1871-1872*, Ch. 260; for arguments in behalf of state aid see *Lexington Observer and Reporter*, 20 June 1866; Lexington *Kentucky Statesman*, 12, 19 March 1851, 15 January 1867, 23 March, 14 May 1869; *Georgetown Weekly Times*, 28 December 1870; *Frankfort Commonwealth*, 20 January 1871; *Paris True Kentuckian*, 20 December 1871.

2. Basil W. Duke, *The Commercial and Railroad Development of Kentucky* (Frankfort, 1887); Carl B. Boyd, Jr., "Local Aid to Railroads in Central Kentucky, 1850-1891" (master's thesis, University of Kentucky, 1963), pp. 3-4.

3. *Slack* v. *Maysville and Lexington R.R. Co.*, 52 Ky. 1 (1852). Judge Elijah Hise issued a long dissenting opinion; ibid., pp. 31-118. While most observers after 1860 did not question the constitutionality of local aid to internal improvements after *Slack*, Governor J. Proctor Knott wrote in 1886 that "as an original proposition it might be well contended that [such aid] is totally without constitutional sanction." *H. J.*, *1885-1886*, p. 1158.

4. For reports of railroad meetings see Lexington *Kentucky Statesman*, 1 January, 10 May 1851, 11, 14 May 1869; *Frankfort Commonwealth*, 30 December 1851; *Bardstown Herald*, 11 February 1852; *London Mountain Echo*, 13 April 1877.

5. For examples of statutes concerning proposed county court railroad subscriptions, see *Acts, 1850-1851*, Chs. 163, 429; *Acts, 1851-1852*, Ch. 297. The Court of Appeals upheld the validity of statutes authorizing subscriptions by only parts of counties. *County Judge of Shelby County* v. *The Shelby Railroad Company*, 68 Ky. 225 (1868); *Allison* v. *Louisville, Harrod's Creek & Westport Ry. Co.*, 72 Ky. 247 (1872).

6. Lexington *Kentucky Statesman*, 9 July 1851, 28 November 1854, 26 April 1870; Lexington *Kentucky Gazette*, 9 February 1870; *Paris True Kentuckian*, 7 February 1872.

7. *Paris True Kentuckian*, 30 April 1870; Lexington *Kentucky Statesman*, 4 January, 2 May, 9 July, 23 August 1851; *Paris True Kentuckian*, 31 January 1872; *Cynthiana News*, 20 May 1869; *Berryman* v. *Trustees of the Cincinnati Southern Railway*, 77 Ky. 755 (1879); Lexington *Kentucky Statesman*, 26 July, 26 August 1851; *Paris True Kentuckian*, 7 August 1871.

8. Lexington *Kentucky Statesman*, 26 March, 9 September 1851, 9 November 1858, 9 August 1867, 30 July 1868; *Georgetown Weekly Times*, 2 August 1871; *Paris True Kentuckian*, 4 August 1869, 9 March 1870, 10 January, 1 May 1872; *Paris Western Citizen*, 26 April 1870, 15 February, 30 April 1872; *Louisville Courier-Journal*, 21 July 1890; Frankfort *Kentucky Yeoman*, 30 April 1881; *Lexington Leader*, 8 June, 13, 27 July, 5 August 1890; *Acts, 1875-1876*, Ch. 866; *Kentucky Union Railroad Company* v. *Bourbon County*, 85 Ky. 98 (1887).

9. *Paris True Kentuckian*, 24 February 1869; *Frankfort Commonwealth*, 3 June 1851; Lexington *Kentucky Statesman*, 21 February 1854; *Lexington Observer and Reporter*, 27 June 1855; *London Mountain Echo*, 9 March, 13 July 1877, 22 August 1879; *Mt. Sterling Democrat*, 19 March 1886.

10. Frankfort *Kentucky Yeoman*, 17 May 1881; L. L. Robinson, *Railroad Statistics . . . to the Voters of Mason County* (Maysville, Ky., 1850), p. 3; Lexington *Kentucky Statesman*, 19 February, 5 March 1851; *Paris True Kentuckian*, 24 February, 8 November 1869.

11. Robinson, *Railroad Statistics*, pp. 4-5; Lexington *Kentucky Statesman*, 26 March 1851, 13 March 1860, 21 May 1867.

12. Lexington *Kentucky Statesman*, 2, 5 September 1851; *Cynthiana News*, 21 July 1853; William C. Ireland, *Elizabethtown, Lexington & Big*

Sandy R.R. . . . *In Opposition to the Proposed Subscription* (Ashland, Ky., 1871), pp. 1-7; *Paris True Kentuckian*, 2, 7 August 1871; Frankfort *Kentucky Yeoman*, 25 January, 1 February 1881, 29 October 1885.

13. *Paris True Kentuckian*, 7 August 1871, 7, 21 February 1872; *Cynthiana News*, 25 December 1873.

14. Lexington *Kentucky Statesman*, 26 March, 25 June 1851, 17, 28 November 1854, 2 February 1856, 30 June 1857, 30 April 1858; *Lexington Observer and Reporter*, 24 November 1858.

15. Lexington *Kentucky Statesman*, 26 March, 25 June, 9 September, 30 April 1858, 7 October, 15, 22 November 1859; *Frankfort Commonwealth*, 3 June 1851; *Paris True Kentuckian*, 3 June, 14 October 1868, 24 February, 17 March, 4, 7 August 1869.

16. Lexington *Kentucky Statesman*, 29 July 1853, 22 May 1860.

17. Lexington *Kentucky Statesman*, 9 August, 15 October 1867, 16 July, 6 August 1869, 24 March, 27 October 1871, 4 March 1873; *Paris True Kentuckian*, 4 October 1871; *Lexington Weekly Press*, 22 October 1873, 20 December 1874, 25 June 1875, 7 May 1876, 25 June 1879; *Winchester Sun*, 20, 27 June, 8 July 1875; *Lexington Leader*, 7 July 1890; Duke, *The Commercial and Railroad Development of Kentucky*, pp. 38-39.

18. *Paris True Kentuckian*, 2 August 1871.

19. Ibid., 23, 30 August, 13, 20 December 1871.

20. *Lexington Observer and Reporter*, 23 December 1871; *Georgetown Weekly Times*, 14 February 1872; *Paris True Kentuckian*, 3, 10, 24, 31 January, 7, 14 February 1872.

21. *Paris True Kentuckian*, 15, 21 February, 3, 10 April, 1 May 1872; Bourbon County Court Order Book (1870-1875), p. 223; Boyd, "Local Aid to Railroads," pp. 36-37.

22. *Frankfort Commonwealth*, 2 September 1870; Frankfort *Kentucky Yeoman*, 6 April 1869, 17 September 1872, 6 January, 30 April, 10, 17 May 1881, 13 October 1883; *Paris True Kentuckian*, 14 October 1874; *London Mountain Echo*, 29 November 1878.

23. Otto A. Rothert, *A History of Muhlenberg County* (Louisville, 1913), pp. 368-74.

24. *Acts, 1877-1878*, Ch. 519; Muhlenberg County Court Order Book (1876-1883), pp. 531-41; ibid. (1883-1889), pp. 89, 491, 501, 505-9, 607, 612; ibid. (1889-1893), pp. 46, 88-89, 121, 123, 125, 142, 304, 306, 309, 345, 591; ibid. (1893-1898), pp. 214, 242, 250-51; ibid. (1898-1904), p. 329; Rothert, *Muhlenberg County*, pp. 376-79.

25. Frankfort *Kentucky Yeoman*, 27 February 1873, 29 January 1881; Marion County Court Order Book (1874-1879), pp. 17, 144, 249, 354, 442, 596; ibid. (1879-1883), pp. 114, 197, 249, 405, 579; ibid. (1883-1887), pp. 134, 308, 466, 630; ibid. (1887-1890), pp. 255, 561-62; *Hickman Courier*, 28 February 1879; *Louisville Evening Post*, 13 February 1879; *Post v. Taylor County*, Federal Cases No. 11, 302 (1879);

Thompson v. *Allen County*, 115 U.S. Reports 550 (1885); Rothert, *Muhlenberg County*, p. 379.

26. *Hardin County* v. *Louisville and Nashville Railroad*, 92 Ky. 412 (1893); Hardin County Court Order Book (1860-1865), pp. 421-23; McCracken County Court Order Book (1855-1861), pp. 9-12; *Greenup County* v. *Maysville and Big Sandy Railroad*, 88 Ky. 659 (1889); *Applegate* v. *Ernst*, 66 Ky. 648 (1868); *Acts, 1875-1876*, Ch. 785; *Louisville and Nashville Railroad* v. *Commonwealth*, 85 Ky. 198 (1887). On 23 January 1885 Governor J. Proctor Knott vetoed a bill exempting the Cincinnati, Green River & Nashville Railroad from Lincoln County taxes for a period of thirty years; *H. J., 1883-1884*, pp. 208-10. Railroad attorney and former governor, John Whyte Stevenson, wrote General Basil W. Duke of the Kentucky Central Railroad in 1884 that he could permit the sale of a railroad bridge to Pendleton County, but under no circumstances should he use the sale price as a credit against a disputed tax judgment, since it was being appealed and since it might jeopardize future efforts to resist county taxation; Stevenson to Duke, 22 November 1884, John Whyte Stevenson Papers, Letterbook 1882-1885, 58M3, King Library Special Collections, University of Kentucky.

27. Frankfort *Kentucky Yeoman*, 24 February, 23 March, 30 September 1869, 24 July 1880; Lexington *Kentucky Gazette*, 2 April 1879.

28. *Cynthiana News*, 3 January 1856, 22 August 1867, 30 July, 1 October 1868; *Frankfort Capital*, 24 April 1886.

29. Frankfort *Commonwealth*, 19, 23 March 1879, 8 April, 25 November, 23 December 1870, 7 February 1872; Frankfort *Kentucky Yeoman*, 23 March, 30 September 1870.

30. Frankfort *Commonwealth*, 15 March 1867; Frankfort *Kentucky Yeoman*, 25 April 1872, 17 November 1874, 2 May, 9 May, 16 November 1876, 3, 5 April 1877, 16 April 1878, 31 July, 16 August, 8 November 1879.

31. *Acts, 1877-1878*, Ch. 148; *Winchester and Mt. Sterling Turnpike Road Co.* v. *Clark County Court*, 60 Ky. 140 (1860); *Kenton County Court* v. *Bank Lick Turnpike Co.*, 73 Ky. 529 (1874); Frankfort *Kentucky Yeoman*, 30 September 1869, 31 May 1881; Lexington *Kentucky Gazette*, 17 April 1878; Lexington *Kentucky Statesman*, 19 February, 13 August 1867; *Cynthiana News*, 14 October 1869, 5 June 1873; *Acts, 1877-1878*, Ch. 544; *Simpson County Court* v. *Arnold*, 70 Ky. 353 (1870).

32. Lexington *Kentucky Gazette*, 25 September, 9 October 1867; *Paris True Kentuckian*, 21 February 1872.

33. Lexington *Weekly Press*, 8, 15, 22 May 1878, 26 March 1879, 7 May, 2 July 1884, 18 February, 27 May, 10 June 1885, 23 February 1887, 20 March 1889; Lexington *Kentucky Gazette*, 14 May, 7 June 1879; *Lexington Leader*, 23, 28 July, 5 August 1890; Thomas D. Clark, *Kentucky: Land of Contrasts* (New York, 1968), pp. 85-93.

34. Stanton, *Revised Statutes*, 2: 289-92; *Debates*, 4: 4924.

35. *Debates*, 4: 4927-28, 4932-34.
36. *Cynthiana News*, 7 October 1869; *London Mountain Echo*, 10 December 1875, 7 September 1883, 5 November 1889; *Hickman Courier*, 30 November 1877; Frankfort *Kentucky Yeoman*, 24 March 1877; Lexington *Kentucky Gazette*, 28 October 1876; *Carver v. Commonwealth*, 75 Ky. 264 (1876); *Ayars v. Cox*, 73 Ky. 201 (1874).
37. Frankfort *Kentucky Yeoman*, 10 August 1854, 17 July 1866; Frankfort *Commonwealth*, 10 August 1866; *Paris True Kentuckian*, 9 August 1866; *Maysville Bulletin*, 9 August 1877; *Lexington Observer and Reporter*, 12 December 1866; *Louisville Courier-Journal*, 31 January 1890; *Debates*, 4: 4927-28, 4932-34.
38. *Lexington Observer and Reporter*, 24 February 1869; Frankfort *Kentucky Yeoman*, 17 October 1867, 22 January 1868, 4 May 1875, 19 August 1876, 12 March, 16 June, 25 July 1885; *Paris True Kentuckian*, 10 November 1875.
39. Lexington *Kentucky Gazette*, 11 August 1868, 3 April 1869, 4 May 1870; *Lexington Observer and Reporter*, 20 March, 8 May 1869; *Lexington Daily Press*, 13 February 1875; *Lexington Transcript*, 12 July 1879, 27 January, 9 August 1882, 26, 28 July 1885; *London Mountain Echo*, 5 November 1889; Barren County Court Order Book (1857-1863), pp. 47, 158, 236, 265, 357; Daviess County Court Order Book (1874-1879), pp. 27, 93; *Acts, 1873*, Chs. 567, 571; *Acts, 1879-1880*, Ch. 907; *Acts, 1883-1884*, Chs. 942, 1164, 1221.
40. Frankfort *Kentucky Yeoman*, 23 December 1865, 10 September 1867, 11, 12 January 1869, 23 January, 16 February, 27 April 1871; *Mercer and Garrard County Courts v. Kentucky River Navigation Companies*, 71 Ky. 300 (1871); Lewis N. Dembitz, *Kentucky Jurisprudence* (Louisville, 1890), pp. 96-97; *Jessamine County v. Swigert's Adm'r*, 8 Ky. L. Rep. 692 (1887).
41. *Debates*, 1: 85-86, 129, 130, 135, 162-64, 178, 189-90, 195, 255, 264, 407-8, 418-28, 527, 759; 2: 2122-24, 2144-47, 2385, 2580-602, 2641-75, 2769-72, 2782-87, 2932-34, 2949-57; 3: 3917, 3989-4024, 4315-18; 4: 5224-31, 5376-84; Constitution of 1891, secs. 157-59.

Chapter 8

1. Stanton, *Revised Statutes*, 1: 328.
2. Ibid., 1: 295, 2: 251-58.
3. Ibid., 1: 295-96.
4. *Debates*, 2: 2392, 2676-77, 2681, 2683-86.
5. *Debates*, 2: 2392, 2675-88, 2787-91; W. C. McChord, *Report on the Financial Condition of Washington County* . . . (Lebanon, 1879); *London Mountain Echo*, 12 November 1875.
6. *Acts, 1853-1854*, Ch. 255; *Acts, 1865-1866*, Ch. 180.
7. *Hickman Courier*, 26 January, 9, 16 February 1877; *Barbourville Mountain Echo*, 16 April 1876; *H. J., 1867-1868*, p. 198; Mt. Olivet

Robertson County Tribune, 12 April 1883; Cynthiana News, 16 February 1854; London Mountain Echo, 11 November 1885.
   8. Acts, 1861-1863, Ch. 421; H. J., 1873-1874, pp. 26-27; H. J., 1883-1884, pp. 19-21; H. J., 1885-1886, p. 22.
   9. Falmouth Independent, 6, 20 March 1879.
   10. Ibid., 4 January 1877.
   11. Ibid.
   12. Ibid., 11, 18 January, 1 March 1877.
   13. Ibid., 15, 29 March, 5 April 1877.
   14. Ibid., 10, 17 May 1877.
   15. Ibid., 12 July, 20 September, 22, 29 November 1877.
   16. Ibid., 2, 9, 16, 23, 30 August, 6 December 1877.
   17. Ibid., 7 February, 7, 21 March, 11 April, 9, 23 May 1878.
   18. Ibid., 6, 13 June 1878, 13 February, 20 March, 24 April, 8 May 1879; Covington Commonwealth, 16 January 1880.
   19. Lexington Observer and Reporter, 26 June, 3 November 1869; Orphan Society of Lexington v. Fayette County, 69 Ky. 413 (1869); Lexington Kentucky Gazette, 25 May 1889.
   20. Lee v. Pendleton County Court, 14 Ky. 159 (1892); Cynthiana News, 30 January, 6 February 1868, 13 April 1871; Mt. Olivet Robertson County Tribune, 26 November, 16 December 1875; Frankfort Kentucky Yeoman, 28 November 1885.
   21. Pusey v. Meade County Court, 64 Ky. 217 (1866); Rodman v. Justices of LaRue County, 66 Ky. 144 (1867); Nelson County Court v. Town of Bardstown, 7 Ky. L. Rep. 41 (1885); Weis v. Lawrence County Court, 13 Ky. L. Rep. 975 (1892).
   22. Bullitt and Feland, General Statutes (1888), p. 342.
   23. Maysville Bulletin, 16, 30 January 1879; Covington Commonwealth, 2 December 1879; Acts, 1887-1888, Ch. 810; Frankfort Capital, 10 January 1885; Fields v. Commonwealth, 14 Ky. L. Rep. 207 (1892).
   24. Stanford Interior Journal, 14 February 1873; Barbourville Mountain Echo, 20 November 1874; Louisville Courier-Journal, 15 February 1891; Acts, 1871, Ch. 1253; Acts, 1873-1874, Ch. 584; Acts, 1875-1876, Chs. 819, 906; Acts, 1877-1878, Ch. 74; Acts, 1885-1886, Ch. 326; Acts, 1887-1888, Ch. 810.
   25. Harvey Myers, ed., A Digest of the General Laws of Kentucky . . . (Frankfort, 1866), p. 124; London Mountain Echo, 12 November 1875; Frankfort Kentucky Yeoman, 30 November 1875, 19 May 1877, 13 November 1879; Lexington Weekly News, 25 June 1876; Acts, 1871-1872, Ch. 156.
   26. The eleven counties were Kenton, Greenup, Magoffin, Carter, Boyd, Floyd, Pendleton, Boone, Owen, Martin, and Knott. Jefferson County adopted a commission system to work out certain city-county problems. For examples of statutes establishing commissions, see Acts, 1879-1880, Ch. 575; Acts, 1881-1882, Ch. 1267; Acts, 1887-1888, Chs. 729, 873.
   27. Covington Commonwealth, 9 January 1880; Frankfort Capital, 2,

30 September, 18 November 1890; *Louisville Courier-Journal*, 15 February 1891; Constitution of 1891, sec. 144.

28. Auditor's Report, Leg. Doc. No. 1, *Kentucky Documents, 1880*, 3: xiii-xiv; Auditor's Report, Leg. Doc. No. 1, *Kentucky Documents, 1883*, 1: viii; Auditor's Report, Leg. Doc. No. 6, *Kentucky Documents, 1885*, 1: viii-ix; Auditor's Report, Leg. Doc. No. 13, *Kentucky Documents, 1887*, 1: v; Auditor's Report, Leg. Doc. No. 3, *Kentucky Documents, 1889*, 2: vi-viii; Auditor's Report, Leg. Doc. No. 19, *Kentucky Documents, 1891*, 2: viii; *Acts, 1881-1882*, Ch. 1453; *Acts, 1889-1890*, Ch. 1754. The hoary doctrine of sovereign immunity did allow counties to resist further encroachment on their often beleaguered budgets. The Court of Appeals ruled, for example, that counties were not liable for injuries sustained to an eight-year-old boy for walking off an unrailed second floor courthouse veranda, for flood damage to a petitioner's property caused by an obstruction of a stream due to county jail construction, for injuries to a plaintiff caused by falling through a courthouse floor into a privy vault, or for the trespass of a road surveyor and his crew onto a plaintiff's property resulting in the destruction of fences, trees, fruit, grass, kale, and potatoes. *Sheppard* v. *Pulaski County*, 13 Ky. L. Rep. 672 (1892); *Downing* v. *Mason County*, 10 Ky. L. Rep. 105 (1888); *Mobley* v. *Carter County* , 12 Ky. Op. 485 (1884); *Hutchinson* v. *Pulaski County Court*, 11 Ky. L. Rep. 117 (1889).

29. For example see Bullitt and Feland, *General Statutes* (1888), pp. 150-51, 458-79.

30. *Debates*, 3: 4130, 4133, 4196-98, 4230-35, 4370-77; *Louisville Evening Post*, 4, 8 February, 17 May 1879, 17, 29 January 1880; Lexington *Kentucky Gazette*, 29 January 1879.

31. *Louisville Evening Post*, 30 November 1878, 4 February 1879; *Debates*, 3: 4234, 4236.

32. *Maysville Bulletin*, 30 August 1877, 7 February 1878; *Maysville Republican*, 1 September 1877; *Hickman Courier*, 5, 12, 19 April 1878; Lexington *Kentucky Gazette*, 30 June, 7, 14 July 1875, 1 January, 18 June 1876; *Cynthiana News*, 6 April, 7 December 1871; *Falmouth Independent*, 14 February 1878; *Stanford Interior Journal*, 18 July 1874.

33. For examples of fee-bill statutes see *Acts, 1865*, Ch. 1240; *Acts, 1867*, Ch. 1826. For examples of salary disputes see *R. Gudgell* v. *Bath County Court*, 10 Ky. Op. 780 (1880); *Ohio County* v. *Newton*, 79 Ky. 267 (1881); *Carpenter* v. *Warnock, Adm'r*, 10 Ky. L. Rep. 934 (1889).

Chapter 9

1. [H. S. Gilbertson], *County Government in Kentucky: A Report by the Efficiency Commission of Kentucky* (Frankfort, 1923), pp. 84-88; John W. Manning, *The Government of Kentucky* (Lexington, 1938), pp. 151-53; Kenneth E. Vanlandingham, *The Fee System in Kentucky Counties* (Lexington, 1951); Vanlandingham, *The Constitution and Local Gov-*

ernment, Kentucky Legislative Research Commission Informational Bulletin No. 36 (1964), pp. 17-19; *Louisville Courier-Journal*, 10 November 1974.

2. [Gilbertson], *County Government*, pp. 35-36; *Louisville Courier-Journal*, 6 November 1975. Following the constitutional amendment, Governor Julian Carroll appointed a Special Advisory Commission on County Government to propose changes in county government to facilitate and complement judicial reform. The commission's recommendations concerned not only the offices of county judge and justice of the peace, but other county offices as well. The General Assembly was scheduled to act on the commission's recommendations at a special session late in 1976. *Louisville Courier-Journal*, 12 September 1976.

3. [Gilbertson], *County Government*, p. 33; Manning, *The Government of Kentucky*, p. 154; *Acts, 1942*, Ch. 115; *Acts, 1948*, Ch. 80. Regulation and lawlessness also spilled over into the twentieth century; *Louisville Courier-Journal*, 1 September 1933, 14, 22 August, 3 September, 5 November 1975. The Special Advisory Commission on County Government proposed creating a Chief Law Enforcement Officer for each county and restricting the sheriff to his tax-collecting duties. *Louisville Courier-Journal*, 9 September 1976.

4. Ibid., pp. 38-40.

5. Ibid., pp. 38, 40-41, 52-53.

6. Ibid., pp. 55-56; Manning, *The Government of Kentucky*, pp. 163-64; Vanlandingham, *The Constitution and Local Government*, p. 22; *Louisville Courier-Journal*, 4 July 1930.

7. [Gilbertson], *County Government*, pp. 41-43, 49-50; Manning, *The Government of Kentucky*, pp. 162-63; *Louisville Courier-Journal*, 13 January 1934, 25 May 1948.

8. [Gilbertson], *County Government*, p. 60; Manning, *The Government of Kentucky*, p. 162; Vanlandingham, *The Constitution and Local Government*, pp. 22-25; *Louisville Courier-Journal*, 1 February 1933, 3 November 1940, 22 January, 2 November 1941, 14 July 1949.

9. [Gilbertson], *County Government*, pp. 68-71, 75; Manning, *The Government of Kentucky*, p. 158.

10. [Gilbertson], *County Government*, pp. 90-91; Manning, *The Government of Kentucky*, pp. 147, 150; Vanlandingham, *The Constitution and Local Government*, pp. 11-12; *Louisville Courier-Journal*, 3 January 1933.

11. *Louisville Courier-Journal*, 8, 10 March 1931, 8 May 1933.

12. Ibid., 30 December 1931, 21, 24 February 1933; *Bowling Green Times-Journal* as reported in the *Courier-Journal*, 18 September 1935; *Carlisle County News* as reported in the *Courier-Journal*, 3 October 1935.

13. *Louisville Courier-Journal*, 13 April 1932, 24 December 1935, 30 September 1951.

14. Ibid., 16 October 1937, 19 June 1940, 3 April 1941, 22 January 1954, 14 June 1965; *H. J., 1954*, pp. 393, 417; Ireland, *County Courts*,

pp. 169-70; *Lexington Herald*, 8 November 1972. In 1938 the Research Division of the Kentucky Legislative Council in cooperation with the W.P.A. issued a report supporting the feasibility of county consolidation; Kentucky Legislative Council, *County Consolidation* (Frankfort, 1938). In 1975 Boyd County voters overwhelmingly rejected a proposed merger of the governments of Ashland, Catlettsburg, and Boyd County; *Louisville Courier-Journal*, 1 September, 5 November 1975.

15. H. S. Gilbertson, *The County: The 'Dark Continent' of American Politics* (New York, 1917); *Louisville Courier-Journal*, 14 June 1965, 17 July 1966; Kenneth Vanlandingham to the Editor, *Louisville Courier-Journal*, 8 December 1974; Clark, *Kentucky*, pp. 162-63.

AN ESSAY ON SOURCES

Basic to any study of the local Kentucky constitution are the county court order books and minute books and court of claims books (only a few counties possessed the latter), which contain summaries of the business of the principal institutions of local government. King Library Special Collections, University of Kentucky, houses microfilm of most of the relevant documents. Originals of these documents may be found either in the relevant county courthouse or in the Kentucky Division of Archives and Records, Frankfort. The published reports of the Court of Appeals are found in the *Kentucky Reports*, the *Kentucky Law Reporter*, and *Kentucky Opinions*. Cases concerning counties are digested in J. Barbour's *Kentucky Digest* . . . , 4 vols. (Louisville, 1878-1897). Federal court decisions about county problems may be found in *Federal Cases*, *United States Reports* and the Federal Circuit Court Order Books in the Federal Archives and Records Center in Chicago.

Legislative *Acts*, *House* and *Senate Journals*, and Legislative *Documents* possess a wealth of information about the operations, duties, and problems of county government and counties in general. Indispensable also are the Constitutions of 1850 and 1891. In conjunction with these compilations, one should consult statutory digests and commentaries, including Richard H. Stanton, ed., *The Revised Statutes of Kentucky* . . . , 2 vols. (Cincinnati, 1860); Harvey Myers, ed., *A Digest of the General Laws of Kentucky* . . . (Frankfort, 1866); Joshua F. Bullitt and John Feland, eds., *The General Statutes of Kentucky* (Frankfort, 1877); Bullitt and Feland, eds., *The General Statutes of*

Kentucky (Louisville, 1888); William B. Allen's Kentucky Officer's Guide and Legal Hand-Book ... (Louisville, 1860) and Richard H. Stanton's A Practical Treatise on the ... Powers and Duties of Justices of the Peace (etc.) ... (Cincinnati, 1875). Also informative about the realities of the local constitution is Lewis N. Dembitz's Kentucky Jurisprudence (Louisville, 1890). Robert M. Bradley's satirical Sketch of Granny Short's Barbecue and the General Statutes of Kentucky (Louisville, 1879) exposes the absurdities of the nineteenth-century Kentucky legislative process.

Especially revealing is the Official Report of the Proceedings and Debates in the Convention Assembled ... September, 1890 to ... Change the Constitution of Kentucky, 4 vols. (Frankfort, 1890). Delegates to this convention spoke candidly about the place of the county in nineteenth-century Kentucky constitutionalism, politics, and society. Freedmen's Bureau Records, Record Group 105 in the National Archives and Records Service contain information essential for an understanding of the confrontation between county and federal government over the black apprenticeship, pauper, and vagrant problems during Reconstruction. Information about the counties in the Civil War can be gleaned from the War of the Rebellion: Official Records of the Union and Confederate Armies, four series, 128 vols. (Washington, D.C., 1880-1901), and the Governors Papers, Kentucky Historical Society, Frankfort. The latter collection contains other information about the counties, but far less than for the period of the first and second constitutions during which the governor possessed far greater powers over county government.

One can gain insights into the counties and internal improvements by reading Basil W. Duke's The Commercial and Railroad Development of Kentucky (Frankfort, 1887); L. L. Robinson's Railroad Statistics: ... to the Voters of Mason County (Maysville, 1850); and William C. Ireland's Elizabethtown, Lexington & Big Sandy R.R. ... In Opposition to the Proposed Subscription (Ashland, Ky., 1871). James Lane Allen's "County

ESSAY ON SOURCES 175

Court Day in Kentucky," *Harper's Magazine* 79 (August 1889): 383-97, is a colorful, if somewhat romanticized, account of nineteenth-century Kentucky's most festive day of the month. W. C. McChord's *Report on the Financial Condition of Washington County* (Lebanon, 1879) is helpful in understanding the chaos of county finances.

Of special significance is the wealth of information contained in nineteenth-century Kentucky newspapers, the most useful of which are the Lexington *Daily Press*, Lexington *Weekly Press*, Lexington *Kentucky Gazette*, Lexington *Kentucky Statesman*, Lexington *Observer and Reporter*, Lexington *Leader*, Lexington *Transcript*, Louisville *Journal*, Louisville *Evening Post*, Louisville *Courier-Journal*, Louisville *Courier*, Louisville *Daily Democrat*, Louisville *Daily Commercial*, Frankfort *Commonwealth*, Frankfort *Kentucky Yeoman*, Frankfort *Capital*, Frankfort *Roundabout*, Covington *Commonwealth*, Barbourville *Mountain Echo*, London *Mountain Echo*, Mt. Olivet *Robertson County Tribune*, Stanford *Interior Journal*, Hickman *Courier*, Falmouth *Independent*, Paris *True Kentuckian*, Paris *Western Citizen*, Cynthiana *News*, Georgetown *Weekly Times*, Winchester *Sun*, Danville *Kentucky Tribune*, Maysville *Bulletin*, Maysville *Republican*, and Bardstown *Herald*. The *New York Times* contains incisive commentary on postbellum Kentucky politics and society.

Collections of personal papers providing glimpses into various aspects of the county include the Martin Cox Papers, the Brutus Clay Papers, the Perry Family Papers, and the John Whyte Stevenson Papers, all located in King Library Special Collections, University of Kentucky, the former two on microfilm.

My earlier study deals with the antebellum antecedents of nineteenth-century Kentucky county government in *The County Courts in Antebellum Kentucky* (Lexington, 1972). Two of the best county histories are B. O. Gaines's *History of Scott County*, 2 vols (Georgetown, Ky., 1906), and Otto A. Rothert's *A History of Muhlenberg County* (Louisville, 1913), the latter containing a useful summary of the Muhlenberg County railroad debt war. Other studies relating to specific problems of nineteenth-century Kentucky counties are Charles Chauncy Binney, "Restrictions on Special and Local Legislation," *American Law Register*, n.s. 32 (1894): 613-32, 721-45, 816-57, 922-43, 1019-33, 1109-61; Lyman H. Cloe and Sumner Marcus, "Special and Local Legislation," *Kentucky Law Journal* 24 (May 1936): 349-86; E. Merton Coulter, *Civil War and Readjustment in Kentucky* (Chapel Hill, N.C., 1926); Allen W. Trelease, *White Terror: The Ku Klux Klan Conspiracy and Southern Reconstruction* (New York, 1971); Harold Wilson Coates, *Stories of Kentucky Feuds* (Knoxville, 1923); and Carl B. Boyd, Jr., "Local Aid to Railroads in Central Kentucky, 1850-1891" (master's thesis, University of Kentucky, 1963).

Illuminating some of the problems and realities of twentieth-century Kentucky counties are H. S. Gilbertson, *County Government in Kentucky: A Report by the Efficiency Commission of Kentucky* (Frankfort, 1923); John W. Manning, *The Government of Kentucky* (Lexington, 1938); Kenneth E. Vanlandingham, *The Constitution and Local Government*, Kentucky Legislative Research Commission Informational Bulletin No. 36 (1964). Gilbertson's *County Government* (New York, 1917) is an important study of early twentieth-century county government in America.

Thomas D. Clark's *Kentucky: Land of Contrasts* (New York, 1968) is the finest treatment of twentieth-century Kentucky and contains incisive comments on previous centuries as well. Published too late for use in this book was Ralph A. Wooster's *Politicians, Planters, and Plain Folk: Courthouse and Statehouse in the Upper South, 1850-1860* (Knoxville, 1975).

INDEX

Adair County, 45, 65
Allen, James Lane, 90, 98
Allen, William B.: *Kentucky Officers' Guide and Legal Handbook*, 28
Allen County, 115
American party (Know-Nothings): success of, in county elections, 43-44; election tactics of, 52-53
apprentices, black: and counties, 64-68
appropriations and expenditures (county), 132-37
assessor (county): duties of, 37-38, 124-25; and Constitution of 1891, 143
attorney, commonwealth. *See* commonwealth attorney
attorney, county. *See* county attorney
auditor (state), 25-26, 137-38

Ballard County, 2, 5
Barren County, 122
Bath County, 2, 110
Beattyville, Ky., 4-5
Bell County, 46
Berea, Ky., 2
Blackburn, Luke P., governor, 82
Blandville, Ky., 5
Boone County, 65
Boone County Recorder, 48
Bourbon County: attempt to form new county from part of, 2; net state revenue of, 3; caliber of county judges of, 23; politics of coroner in, 38; origin of Democratic popular primary in, 55; and black apprentices, 66; and court day, 90-91, 93, 98; and railroads, 104, 106, 111-12; and free turnpikes, 119; assessment of horses in, 128
Bowling Green Times-Journal, 149
Boyd County, 85, 128
Boyle County: dispute with Garrard County, 17; election-day fighting in, 52; and black apprentices, 67; and railroads, 104, 109
Boyle County Circuit Court, 17
Bracken County: Civil War financial burdens of, 3; county elections of 1890, 47-48; and taxation, 126, 128
Bradley, Robert M.: *A Sketch of Granny Short's Barbecue and the General Statutes of Kentucky*, 10
Bramlette, Thomas, governor, 62
Breathitt County, 73
Breckinridge County, 17
Buckner, Simon B., governor: and crime problem in counties, 79-80, 84-86
buildings (county), 121-22

Calloway County, 3
Campbell County: net state revenue of, 3; relations with Newport, 16; special police force authorized for, 88; taxpayers' revolt in, 128
Carlisle County, 2
Carlisle County News, 149
Carter County, 85, 110
Chesapeake & Ohio Railroad, 110
Christian County, 67
Cincinnati Southern Railroad, 104
circuit courts, Kentucky, 81-82, 137-38
city-county relations, 13-16
Civil War and counties, 60-63
claims brokers, 134-35
Clark County: sale of county treasuryship in, 40; Prohibitionist activity in, 52; politics of, 52, 55; and court day, 90-91, 99; and railroads, 104-5, 110
clerk, county. *See* county clerk
commonwealth attorney, 35-36, 81, 143, 145
consolidation (proposed) of counties, 6-8, 143, 148-50
constable, 38-40; and crime control, 78-79; and fraudulent claims, 83; abolition of, advocated, 144
constitutional convention of 1890-1891: restricts local legislation, 13; and probate matters, 21; and lawlessness, 71, 77-78; and road labor tax, 120-21; and county debt limitations, 123; and poll tax, 126; and county commissions, 137
Constitution of 1891, 143
coroner, 38; and crime control, 78-79
county attorney, 35-36; and crime problem, 81, 83; and county claims, 134, 137; fees and salary of, 138, 140; and Constitution of 1891, 143; in the twentieth century, 145, 147
county auditor, 136
county clerk, 33-35; disputed election of, in Madison County, 63; and Pendleton County taxpayers' revolt, 130; and claims brokering, 134; and statement of county finances, 136; fees of, in Jefferson County, 138; in the early twentieth century, 145-46
county commissions, 136-37, 143
county court. *See* county judge; court of claims; specific counties
county judge, 18-24; and Madison County election, 63; and feuds, 73, 76-77; and crime control, 78, 80; and railroad subscriptions, 111-12; and public buildings, 121; and claims brokering, 134; and claims processing, 137; fees and salary of, 138-40; in the twentieth century, 144, 147
county-line changes, 5-6, 152 n.13
county police, 86-89, 144-45
county seats, 4-5
county tax commissioner, 146
court day, 90-100
courthouse gangs, 53-54, 157-58 n.23
courthouses, 121-22
Court of Appeals, Kentucky: and intercounty bridge controversies, 17; and liquor licenses, 22; and naturalization powers of city courts, 22; and liabilities of sheriff, 26; rules on minors as deputy county clerks, 34; on contested election of jailer, 37; invalidates election of female jailer, 40; and vote-buying, 51; and disputed election of county clerk, 63; rules on court day foreclosure sales, 95; upholds railroad subscriptions, 102-3, 106; rules on railroad county-tax liability,

INDEX

116; and road law, 120; invalidates county river improvement subscriptions, 123; rules on claims and taxpayers' disputes, 133-34, 170 n.28
court of claims, 124-37, 146
Covington, Ky., 16, 88
creation of counties, 1-3
crime (and counties), 71-89, 143
Crittenden County, 66
Cumberland & Ohio Railroad, 113, 115
Cumberland County, 45, 66
Cynthiana, Ky., 54
Cynthiana News: supports Democratic popular primary in Harrison County, 58; and court day rivalries, 98-99; supports Harrison County turnpike construction, 117; denounces court of claims, 133

Danville, Ky., 105
Daviess County, 40, 122
Democratic party: success of, in county elections, 42-48; intraparty competition of, 47-49; election tactics of, 52-53; origin of popular primaries of, 53-59

Edmonson County, 144
elections (county), 42-59, 63
Elizabethtown, Lexington & Big Sandy Railroad, 104, 110.
Elizabethtown & Paducah Railroad, 113-14
Estill County, 5-6, 112

Falmouth Independent, 57, 129-31
Farmers' Alliance party, 47
Fayette County: net state revenue of, 3; city-county Democratic split in, 13-14; county judges of, 21, 23; political importance of sheriff in, 28; quality of justices of peace in, 30; politics of jailer and coroner in, 37-38; female deputy county clerk of, 40; county elections in, 43-46, 51; origin of Democratic popular primary of, 55-56; crime problems of, 84, 87-88; and court day, 91-94, 96, 98-100; and railroads, 101, 104-6, 109-10; free turnpike movement in, 118-19; and dilapidated courthouse, 122; and dispute over county judge's salary, 139-40; merges with city of Lexington in 1974, 150
Fayette County Circuit Court, 133
Federal District Court (western district) of Kentucky, 67-68
fees, 83-84, 138-40, 142-44
feuds (and counties), 72-78
Fisk, Clinton B., brigadier general, 64, 69
Fleming County, 1-2, 6
Frankfort, Ky., 105
Frankfort, Paris & Big Sandy Railroad, 105-6, 111-12
Frankfort Commonwealth: reports on county judges, 20; on county politics, 44; on county election of 1858, 53; endorses county railroad investment, 106; supports county turnpike investment, 117
Frankfort Daily Capital, 117, 135
Frankfort Kentucky Yeoman: praises county clerks, 35; describes evolution of sheriffalty, 80; on justices of the peace and crime control, 81; condemns vigilantism, 85
Franklin County: caliber of county judges of, 23; county politics in, 27, 29, 37; performance of a justice of the peace in, 32; county elections of, 52-53; dissatisfaction with Democratic nominating procedures in, 56; and Ku Klux Klan, 72, 79; citizens of,

180   INDEX

Franklin County (continued):
    protest crime, 84; and court day, 90, 99; and railroad investment, 105, 111; and turnpike construction, 117-18; and dilapidated jail, 122
Freedmen's Bureau (and counties), 63-70
French-Eversole feud, 76-77
Fulton County, 122, 126-27

Gallatin County, 46, 97
Garrard County, 17, 123
General Assembly, Kentucky: and county seats, 4; and county-line changes, 5-6; and abolition of counties, 6; and local and special legislation, 8-13; and inter-county disputes, 16-17; and public administrators and guardians, 20-21; and the sheriff's tax-collecting duties, 25; authorizes special tax collectors, 27; and the number of justices of the peace, 29; increases jurisdiction of the justices of the peace, 29-30; and the county clerk, 34; and the county treasurer, 40; and popular primaries, 58-59; and disloyal county officers, 60; and county problems of the Civil War, 61-63; and black apprentices, 64-65; passes poor tax on blacks, 68, 69; almost abolishes Rowan County, 76; and crime control, 81; legislates against fraudulent claims, 84; legislates against lax law enforcement, 85; and proposals to fight county crime, 85-89; temporarily authorizes sale of state turnpike stock, 102, 119; and Muhlenberg County railroad bond controversy, 114; resists assumption of county railroad debts, 115; and railroads' county tax liability, 116; passes turnpike statutes, 117-18; and problems of tax collection, 127; and claims processing, 135-36; creates county commissions, 136-37; and expenses of pauper idiots, 138; reforms county finances, 146
Georgetown Weekly Times, 32-33
Gilbertson, H. S., 143-45, 150
governor of Kentucky, 79-80, 82-83, 85-86. See also individual governors
Granger party, 46
Grant County: and proposed boundary change, 5; county election in 1862, 44; and court day rivalries, 99; taxpayers' revolt in, 128; and dispute over county salaries, 140
Graves, Benjamin F., judge (Fayette County), 21, 23, 132-33
Grayson County, 17, 51
Greenback party (National Greenback Labor party), 47
Green County, 52, 115
Greenup County, 110, 116

Hancock County Circuit Court, 17
Hardin County, 115
Harlan County, 62
Harrison County: county judge and tavern licenses of, 21; exploits of a constable in, 39; Democratic popular primary in, 54, 56, 58; and court day rivalries, 98-99; and turnpikes, 117, 119; opposition to taxation in, 127-28; and dispute over county salaries, 140
Harrodsburg, Ky., 105
Hart County: and party activity in 1858, 43; and county elections of 1878, 47; and authorization to fight Civil War crime, 86
Hawes, Richard, judge (Bourbon County), 66, 111
Hazard, Ky., 76

INDEX

Henrietta County (proposed), 2
Hickman County, 139
Hickman Courier, 54
Hopkins County, 48, 66
horse sales (court day), 93-94
horse shows (court day), 93-94
Howard, O. O., major general, 64
Humphrey, Cook (Rowan County sheriff), 73-74
Huntington, Collis P., 110

Jackson County, 122
jailer, 36-37; elections for, 46-47, 49; and crime control, 78-79; and jail, 121; and fees in Jefferson County, 138; and Constitution of 1891, 143; in the twentieth century, 145
jails, 121-22
Jefferson County: net state revenue of, 3; relations of, with Louisville, 14-16; alleged failures of justices of the peace in, 33; lucrativeness of county clerkship in, 34; contested election of jailer in, 37; exploits of a constable in, 39; Democratic popular primary of, 58-59; and special police force, 86-87; fees of county officers of, 138; and local units of government, 150
Jessamine County, 98-99, 109
judicial amendment of 1975, 144
juries, 82
justice of the peace, 28-33; and crime control, 78, 80-81; and fraudulent claims, 83; and public buildings, 121; and claims brokering, 134; compared to county commissioners, 137; in the twentieth century, 144

Kenton County: net state revenue of, 3; relations of, with Covington, 16; performance of a justice of the peace in, 32; humane conduct of jailer in, 37; county election of 1870, 45; and special police force, 88; taxpayers' revolt in, 128; county commission of, 137
Kentucky River Navigation Company, 122-23
Knott, J. Proctor, governor: and Rowan County feud, 74-76; and Perry County feud, 76-77; urges transfer of crime costs to counties, 84; complains about tax assessments, 127-28
Knox County, 51-52
Knoxville, Ky., 5
Ku Klux Klan, 72

Larue County, 12
Laurel County: caliber of county judges of, 23; conduct of jailer in, 37; and dilapidated courthouse, 122; and taxation, 126-27
Lawrence County, 85
Lee County, 4-5
Leslie, Preston H., governor: and crime problem, 79, 83, 85-86; complains about tax evasion, 127
Leslie County, 122
Letcher County, 61-62
levy (county). *See* poll tax
Lexington, Ky.: and county-city Democratic split, 13-14; and crime, 87-88; and court day, 91-93, 96; and railroads, 104-6, 110
Lexington & Big Sandy Railroad, 110. *See also* Elizabethtown, Lexington & Big Sandy Railroad
Lexington & Covington Railroad, 105, 109
Lexington & Danville Railroad, 105, 109
Lexington *Kentucky Gazette:* proposes county consolidation, 7;

Lexington *Kentucky Gazette:* praises Fayette County judge, 23; criticizes "mad scramble for office," 48-49; defends vigilantism, 85; supports county police force, 87; on Fayette County livestock sales, 91; and Bourbon County court day boastfulness, 98; supports free turnpikes, 118-19; and construction of new courthouse, 122

Lexington *Kentucky Statesman,* 107

Lexington Leader: reports need for city annexation, 16; praises Fayette county judge, 23; reports on voter intimidation in Montgomery County, 51

Lexington Weekly Press: and city-county Democratic split, 14; predicts continuance of vigilantism, 85; endorses free turnpikes, 119

Lincoln County: and elections of 1874, 46; and Civil War crime, 86; and court day attendance, 99; and salary disputes, 140

livestock sales (court day), 90-93

Livingston County, 12

local and special legislation, 8-13, 17, 142

Louisville, Ky., 14-16, 104

Louisville & Nashville Railroad, 104, 115

Louisville Courier-Journal: reports on county elections of 1870, 45; on vote-buying in county elections, 50-51; and Rowan County feud, 75; condemns county lawlessness, 77; on number of counties and state costs, 84; and decline of court day, 100; supports county consolidation, 148

Louisville Democrat, 43

Louisville Evening Post, 82, 139

Louisville Journal, 42

McCracken County: and Civil War disruptions, 61-63; and dispute with railroad, 115-16

McCreary, James B., governor: vetoes bill exempting certain sheriffs, 25; and Breathitt County feud, 73

Madison County, 63

Magoffin, Beriah, governor, 62

Magoffin County, 136-37

Manning, John W., 146, 148

Marion County, 65, 115

Marshall County: attempt to form new county from part of, 2; land awarded to, 3; probate dispute with Hancock County, 17; and claims processing, 135

Mason County: net state revenue of, 3; caliber of county judges of, 23; and county elections of 1874, 46; origin of Democratic popular primary in, 54, 56-58; and railroads, 102-3, 109; and dispute over county judge's salary, 139

Maysville & Big Sandy Railroad, 116

Maysville & Lexington Railroad, 102, 105, 107, 109

Maysville Bulletin: proposes county consolidation, 6-7; condemns local legislation, 9; praises Mason county judges, 23; opposes Democratic popular primary in Mason County, 56-58

Maysville Republican, 56

Meade County, 43, 45

Menifee County, 3

Mercer County: and local legislation, 12; and intercounty railroad rivalry, 105; and river improvement subscription, 123

Mobile & Ohio Railroad, 115-16

Monroe County, 66

Montgomery County: attempt to form new county from part of,

INDEX

2; railroad debt of, 3; election of jailer in 1878, 47; voter intimidation in, 51; and railroad investments, 110
Morehead, Ky., 74
Morgan County, 1-2
Mount Sterling, Ky., 105, 110
Mt. Sterling Democrat, 107
Mt. Sterling Sentinel, 113
Muhlenberg County, 43, 113-15

Nashville & Cincinnati Railroad, 104
Nelson County, 29
Newport, Ky., 16, 88
New York Times: on Kentucky's lawlessness, 71-72, 77, 79; criticizes gubernatorial pardons, 82; and court day socializing, 95-96
Nicholas County: attempt to form new county from part of, 2; murderer from, sentenced leniently, 82; vigilantism in, 85; and court day rivalries, 99
Nicholasville, Ky., 99

officers (county), 18-41. *See also name of specific officer*
Ohio County: election day fighting in, 52; and poor blacks, 68-69; and sheriff, 144
Oldham County, 6
Owen County, 128
Owensboro, Ky., 68
Owingsville, Ky., 105

Paris, Ky.: political influence of, 55; and court day, 98; and railroads, 105-6
Paris & Maysville Railroad, 104
Paris True Kentuckian, 111
Paris Western Citizen, 31
Pendleton County: and proposed boundary change, 5; performance of a justice of the peace in, 32; and elections of 1874,

46; failure of Democratic popular primary in, 57; crime problem in, 79; criminal law enforcement in, 84; taxpayers' revolt in, 128-32; and poor farm site, 133; dispute over salary of county judge and county attorney in, 140
Perry County: length of service of county clerk in, 34; and Civil War disruptions, 62; and feud of, 76-77
police (county), 86-89
police courts, 19, 137
political parties and county elections, 42-49, 53-59; extent of partisanship, 42-47; intraparty competition, 47-49; origins of party primaries, 53-59
poll tax, 125-27
poor blacks (and counties), 68-69
poor laws (and counties), 68-69
posse comitatus, 86
Powell County, 5-6
primary elections, 53-59
Proctor, Ky., 4-5
Prohibitionist party, 47, 49, 52
Pulaski County, 126

quarterly courts. *See* county judge

railroad bonds (county), 113-15
railroads (and counties), 101-16, 142
Reconstruction (and counties), 63-70
Republican party, 44-48
Richland County (proposed), 2
river improvement projects, 122-23
road law, 119-21, 147
Robertson County: special tax of, 3; homicide case in, 80-81; opposition to taxation in, 127; and claims dispute, 133-34
Rockcastle County, 22, 80
Rowan County: creation of, 1-2;

Rowan County (*continued*):
proposed abolition of, 6; vote-buying in, 51; feud in, 73-76; and railroads, 110
Russell County, 65

salaries (county), 138-40
sale of county offices, 50
Scott County: net state revenue of, 3; alleged illegality of two justices of the peace in, 32-33; and court day, 90; and railroads, 106, 111; and free turnpikes, 119
Shelby County, 3, 6
sheriff, 24-28; and Fayette County elections of 1872 and 1874, 45-46; Civil War difficulties of, 61-62; and feuds, 73-77; and crime control, 77-80; and jury selection, 82; and fraudulent claims, 83-84; and attempted repudiation of Marion County railroad debt, 115; as tax collector, 124, 127, 129-32; and claims brokering, 134-35; fees of, in Jefferson County, 138; and Constitution of 1891, 143, 154 n.18; in the twentieth century, 144-47; proposals to remove law enforcement duties of, 171 n.3
Special Advisory Commission on County Government, 171 nn. 2 & 3
Speed, James, 67, 69
Stanford Interior Journal, 22
Stanton, Richard, 81
state police, 144
Stevenson, John Whyte, governor, 12-13
Supreme Court, U.S., 113, 115
surveyor (county), 40

taxation (state and county), 124-32, 146. *See also* poll tax
tax commissioner (county). *See* county tax commissioner
Taylor County, 115
Tolliver-Martin feud, 73-76. *See also* Rowan County
treasurer (county), 40, 146
Trigg County, 2
Trimble County, 122
turnpikes, 116-19

Union County, 121
Union party, 44

vagrants, black (and counties), 69-70
Versailles & Midway Railroad, 104
vigilantism, 71-72, 84-85. *See also* Ku Klux Klan
vote-buying, 50-51

Warren County, 44
Washington County, 113, 126
Wayne County, 65
Whig party, 42
Whitley County, 122, 127
Wickliffe, Ky., 5
Williamstown, Ky., 5
Wolfe County, 61, 100
women in county government positions, 40
Woodford County: net state revenue of, 3; alleged discrimination by two justices of the peace in, 33; and court day, 90, 99; and railroads, 104

Young, Zachery (Rowan county attorney), 74-75

www.ingramcontent.com/pod-product-compliance
Lightning Source LLC
Chambersburg PA
CBHW032045150426
43194CB00006B/425